The Art of Writing & Speaking The English Language

GRAMMAR AND PUNCTUATION

GRAMMAR AND PUNCTUATION

S. CODY

The Readers Paradise
New Delhi - 110002

Grammar and Punctuation
S. Cody

1st Edition

ISBN - 978-93-85958-92-2

Published by
The Readers Paradise
103, 4787/23, Ansari Road,
Darya Ganj, New Delhi - 110002
011-23246222, 09811197091, 9654444181
thereadersparadisesales@gmail.com
www.thereadersparadise.com

Price Rs. 495.00

Typesetting by
Sanya Computers

Printed in India
Balaji Offset, Delhi

Contents

PUNCTUATION

GRAMMAR

1

The Study of Grammar

The subject of grammar* originally included all that we have considered under the head of "Word-study," and also the subject of prosody, or verse-making. It was defined as the art or science of writing and speaking a language correctly in every detail.

In modern usage the meaning of the word has been restricted to accuracy in the relation of words in sentence structure. One writer has defined it as "the science of the sentence." In Latin and Greek the relations of words in sentences were indicated by a system of terminations, and the study of grammar was largely a process of memorizing these terminations. At the bottom of all, however, was a logical relationship between words, which was as fixed and definite as the laws of mathematics; and an intelligent and literary use of the language required a full appreciation of this word-logic. In English the terminations have nearly all been lost, and the essential logic of sentence structure has become the main thing. Of course this means that we must abandon the methods useful in teaching Latin and Greek grammar, and formulate a system which shall approach the subject from just the opposite side.

---

*The word grammar is derived from the Greek *gramma,* a letter, and so meant minute accuracy in writing.

Usage determines the meanings and values of words, and to some extent our habits of arranging words; but quite apart from usage, words have a fixed logical relationship to each other in the sentence, and this logical relationship is something that usage or custom can never interfere with or affect in any way. Hence grammar may properly be called a "science," since it is subject to fixed principles.

By universal consent, however, the study of grammar has always been made to include a study of the peculiar word-formations connected with the relationships of words in sentences, and of course all word-forms, even those which mark grammatical relationships, are constantly affected by usage.

It is only by studying grammar as "the science of the logical relationships of words in sentences," however, that we shall ever get a universal key to absolutely correct expression of our ideas in words.

As correct spelling and pronunciation depend largely upon training the eye and training the ear to accurate observation of sound and form, so correct sentence-structure depends upon training the mind to habits of care and logical accuracy in making sentences. Unless our mind is able to think with precision, we can never hope to write or speak with precision. The memorizing of rules and definitions, too often supposed to be "study of grammar," will have no effect whatever on the accuracy with which we use words. But if we can cultivate a habit of care and accuracy in thinking, even if we do not pay any attention whatever to the technical details of grammar, we shall doubtless make accurate writers and speakers.

The teaching of grammar in our schools has undoubtedly been very much misdirected. Little or no attention has been paid to training the mind of the pupil in logical, accurate thinking, and the mastery of a mere system is useful to none except those who have to pass examinations. Ask any teacher, "Did you ever teach a pupil to write and speak grammatically by trying to teach him the subject of grammar from a textbook?" The answer will invariably be that correct writers and speakers were never made in this way. The persistent correction of errors in composition exercises has been the chief means of practical improvement.

The mature student who takes up the study of grammar (and many are doing it) rarely has any other object in view than to improve his use of the language. "When he finds that digging away on the "system" called grammar does not help him one iota, of course he becomes discouraged. He desires practical skill, not theory.

Theoretical knowledge of grammar is useful if it furnishes us the means of testing in a critical way the accuracy of a sentence. While we are actually writing we must be guided by instinct and habit, and by these almost solely; but instinct and habit cannot be relied upon entirely, and when it comes to polishing, we should be in a position to test all doubtful points, and be sure that we are right or wrong.

Theory also serves another purpose. A large part of our knowledge of grammar must come from a habit of observing the logical relationships of words in sentences as we read. Our theory or system enables us to associate and classify, and so does much to aid the memory.

The common methods of teaching grammar are open to two other objections. The old fashion was to drill the pupil by setting before him a long list of errors to be corrected. The reasoning was that since we study grammar that we may be able to correct errors in our own writing, we should have plenty of practice in correcting errors in the writing of other people. We lost sight of the fact that while it Is desirable that we be able to correct errors, it is far more desirable that we never make them at all. A familiarity with, and a habit of dealing with, correct forms so that we shall use them instinctively, are far more important than the ability to correct. The habit solely of correcting would lead us to hesitate and analyse at every word, and such a habit would make snobs and pedants of us.

The other objection relates to the kind of material we were given to deal with in the study of words correctly used. In olden times we were expected to "parse" paragraphs from beautiful compositions until we hated everything connected with the subject. This parsing took the form of uttering a lingo or formula in connection with every word in the sentence as we came to it. The lingo soon became almost purely mechanical, and was so often repeated that nearly all its meaning was lost. We sacrificed an interesting study of what we did not know to an endless repetition of that which we did know only too well. Thus all interest was destroyed.

In modern grammars this "parsing" has been reduced to a minimum; but instead of passages from great authors, or entire compositions, we are given hundreds of disconnected sentences. As these sentences are mere illustrations of formulae, they have no interest (or very little) in themselves. It is impossible to turn the attention rapidly from one subject to another; and sentences selected from standard literature have little value, because they are dissociated from the discussion or description of which they form a part. Often they are highly figurative, and for this reason they are even more meaningless than the old-fashioned "made-up" sentences which contained errors.

The grammar of a word depends so entirely upon its meaning that we should never attempt to analyse words from a grammatical point of view except in sentences which we understand perfectly and in which we take a lively interest. That we should be interested in the meaning of the words we are studying is important for many reasons: first, because unless the mind is interested it is never wide awake; and again, because if the meaning is vague or dim our grammatical analysis will at once become mechanical and so lose all its value.

For grammatical study we should therefore select a simple, easy composition in which we can become interested, and one which affords us the best possible models for our instinctive imitation; and then we should study only the words whose relationships are slightly peculiar, and to that extent interesting and useful for study. The mind is sufficiently burdened without wasting time and energy on that which we know already, or on mere mechanical formulae. Such a study as this will create and cultivate the habit of looking out for peculiar word-relationships as we read; and by confining our attention to correct forms, even to masterly forms, we shall gradually acquire the instinct of constructing correctly and instinct will do ten thousands times for us what reason will.

It will be seen that if any mind is incapable of logical

thought, it will be incapable of writing and speaking grammatically, or at any rate of analysing the grammatical structure of a sentence. Other minds will be slow and dull in the study. For the average mind grammar is a hard study, and a subject which can never be completely mastered. It must be the object of life-long effort. We therefore see how much more important it is to form habits than to acquire theories or systems; and the theories or systems acquired should be so simple and natural that they can be easily remembered, or can be worked out anew if forgotten. Moreover, it is unnecessary to burden oneself with a system for analysing that which one knows well already and will never wish to test. The ordinary system of grammar is far too cumbersome to remember easily, and too much burdened with that which has little practical value in improving our skill.

It is really remarkable to what an extent grammar may be simplified for ordinary use. Words may have seven different logical relationships to ideas and to each other as used in a sentence, known as the parts of speech (the logical relationships of the noun and of the pronoun being regarded as the same). These principal relationships have important modifications in the case of nouns and pronouns, and verbs. But here in a nutshell we have practically the whole science of grammar. The few forms to indicate cases of nouns, and number and person of verbs we do not need to learn because we know them already, and all we require is to be able to distinguish those cases in which confusion is possible. It counts for nothing to be able to name all the combinations of words In English which correspond to varying forms in Latin. We also have little use for the names of groups of words, of kinds of sentences, etc. The only thing really required is an understanding of the fundamental logical laws on which words must be united if they are to form perfect sentences. If we know twenty things in grammar the twenty essential things—we may write with entire accuracy without knowing a thousand and one other things taught in books on grammar.

But this simplification of grammar does not mean quite so much as it seems to. We must admit that it is easier to learn the thousand and one useless things than the twenty essentials. Indeed, if we understood the seven fundamental relationships denominated the parts of speech we should probably be excellent grammarians; but few of us ever do fully master even those seven fundamentals of word-logic.* We find it very easy to fall into the mechanical habit of saying "but" is a conjunction, "by" is a preposition, etc.; so of course we are puzzled when "but" is a preposition or an adjective or a noun or a verb, and our system fails us when we come across "by" used as an adverb or the like. The "parts of speech" are not "classes of words", as we have been told, but "classes of logical relationships in sentences,"

* "All language is imperfectly logical," remarks a friendly critic on reading this declaration of principles. That is quite true. As far as the values of words are concerned, language is a purely natural growth. Not only does the same word have many different meanings, but its value in relation to other words is constantly shifting without any logical reason for doing so. These shifting word values we must learn by reading' good books and talking with cultivated people. This natural side of language is illustrated by our idioms. But once we have determined our word values, we must unite our words in sentences for the expression of our thought according to exactly the same laws which govern our thinking, that is, the laws of logical sequence. The present writer has attempted to separate the logical relationship of words in sentences from the changing means and values of those words, to which are due the so called "illogical" phases of grammar.

and nothing on earth will enable us to tell what part of speech any given word is except as we find it in a sentence, or conveying an idea of some kind. The idea which the word conveys is the sole determining factor.

One class of words does convey ideas without assistance, and that is the "name" class—"nouns." Beginning with this class, let us examine the various relationships which other words may have to it and to each other until we have arrived at the complete and perfect *sentence*,—our unit in grammar, just as the *word* is our unit in spelling. This part of our work is fully defined by the term "sentence-study."

2

The Parts of Speech

1. Nouns

In the first paragraph of "Black Beauty"* let us pick out the words that stand for some definite object we can think of. Such words are *meadow, pond, water, trees*; also *place, day-time,* etc. Say nothing but the word *pond,* for instance, and you have in your mind a clear picture of something real.

In the sentences in this passage there are also many other kinds of words, such as *the, remember, about, pleasant, from.* But none of these words means anything definite except in connection with other words. *Pond* calls up the idea of a pond, without any other words with it, but *remember* means nothing unless there is some one or something to remember, and something that is remembered. So *from* and *the* mean nothing except in connection with other words. Even *pleasant* must be connected with some other word in order to have its full

---

* "The first place that I can well remember was a large, pleasant meadow, with a pond of clear water in it. Some shady trees leaned over it, and rushes and water-lilies grew at the deep end. Over the hedge on one side we looked into a plowed field, and on the other we looked over a gate at our master's house, which stood by the roadside. At the top of the meadow was a grove of fir-trees, and at the bottom a running brook overhung by a steep bank."—"Black Beauty," Chapter I.

meaning, as “a pleasant day,” “a pleasant thought,” or the like.

By careful consideration you will see that every word depends on some other word, until you come back to the *noun,* or name-word, which is complete in itself. Each word in a complete sentence has a fixed logical relationship of its own. The study of these logical relationships is the basis of grammar. The starting-point is the noun, which represents a complete idea in itself, and (with the words connected with it) gives us the “subject” (of a sentence). A *sentence* is a complete chain of words, representing a complete thought.

2. Verbs

A noun, as we have said, means something apart from any other word connected with it. But when we say *boy, man, tree, John,* we call up merely a simple picture. If we wish to speak of the boy as running, the man as walking, the tree as growing, John as speaking, we must use a verb. When we say, “The boy runs,” “The man walks,” “The tree grows,” “John speaks,” we make a statement, we assert something to be true. The word that asserts, such as *runs, walks,* or *speaks,* is called a *verb.* A verb also expresses a command, as when we say, “Run, John.”

In participles and infinitives the assertive quality is imperfect, but it still exists. Old grammarians defined verbs as words signifying *to do, to be,* or *to suffer.*

As we shall see later, a verb often comprises several separate words, as *might have done, shall have been done, can be done, is being done,* etc. The verb and the words connected with it are called the “predicate.”

3. Pronouns

There are a number of small words which take the place of nouns. Thus when I speak of myself I do not call myself by name and say, "John runs;" I say "*I* run." If I have once mentioned John's name, so that we know to whom *he* refers, we say, "*He* walks." And if we have been talking about the meadow we may say, "*It* is full of water." These words *I, he, it,* etc., are called pronouns (Latin, *for nouns*). They have just the same relationships as nouns, and the only difficulty in the use of them comes in making it clear to exactly what noun each pronoun refers. The noun to which a pronoun refers is called its *antecedent.*

4. Adjectives

Then there are words which are usually placed before nouns to describe them. When we say, "A large pleasant meadow," *a, large,* and *pleasant,* are descriptive of the noun *meadow.* They are called adjectives. When we say, "The boy is good," *good* is an adjective also, though placed after the verb, because it expresses a quality of the noun *boy. First, last, white, blue, fair, sweet, kind, lovely, hard, bitter, sour,* etc., are all words used to describe nouns,— that is, adjectives, though under some circumstances they may also be other parts of speech.

5. Adverbs

When we say, "The sun shines brightly," "The man strikes hard," "I am heartly pleased to see you," etc., *brightly* modifies *shines, hard* modifies *strikes, heartily* modifies *pleased,* telling sun shines, how the sun shines, how the man strikes, how much I am pleased to see you. These words are called adverbs. When we say, "I am here," "Do you love me now?" "Speak thus," the words *here, now,* and *thus,* expressing place, time, and manner, are also adverbs. Again when we say, "He speaks very plainly," "He draws extremely badly," not only *plainly* and *badly* are adverbs modifying verbs, but *very* and *extremely* are also adverbs, though they modify other adverbs. We also say, "He is a very good boy," "The day is tediously long," "The rose has an exquisitely sweet odor," in which *very, tediously,* and *exquisitely* are adverbs modifying adjectives.

Adverbs are words which modify verbs, adjectives, or other adverbs.

> **Note**—There are many words placed in the predicate near the verb which are not adverbs. We shall find later that these may be "predicate adjectives," "predicate nouns," and nouns which are objects of the verbs.

6. Prepositions

There are also various small words which introduce nouns. Thus we have such phrases as "from the gate," "above the water," "into the sea," "by means of love," etc. The words *from, above, into, by, of,* used to introduce the nouns which follow them and connect them to other nouns and to verbs, etc., are called *prepositions.* A preposition with its noun is called a *phrase.* A phrase that modifies a noun just as an adjective does, is called an *adjective phrase,* and a phrase that modifies a verb just like an adverb, is called an *adverbial phrase.*

A prepositional phrase (there are other kinds of phrases) may have any or all the relationships which an adjective or an adverb may have.

Such phrases as "to go," "to be," "to kill," etc., in which a verb follows the preposition *to,* are called the "infinitive mode of the verb." The *to* is often omitted or implied.

7. Conjunctions

A word that joins together two words or phrases of the same kind, or joins one sentence to another sentence, is called a conjunction. Thus in the sentence. "The boy and the man came here together, but went away separately," *and* is a conjunction joining *boy* and *man*, and *but* joins the two verbs *came* and *went*. When we say, "He will do it if I will let him," *if* is a conjunction joining the subordinate sentence "I will let him" to the main sentence "He will do it." In the complete sentence, "Where I go, there ye shall be also," *where* is a conjunction joining the subordinate sentence "I go" to the main sentence "there ye shall be also." In this case *where* is also an adverb of place. We may call it either an "adverbial conjunction" or a "relative adverb." In this book we follow the common usage and speak of it as a "relative adverb" rather than as a conjunction. *While, when,* etc., are also used in the same way, and so are the relative pronouns *who, which, that,* etc.

8. Interjections

The only other kind of words which we shall find is the interjection. Examples: *Oh! ah! alas!* The interjection stands alone, without direct relationship to other words. We may call it a "sentence word."

We now have a rough classification of the different kinds of relationships which a word may have in a sentence. These relationships are called "the parts of speech." A word will sometimes have one relationship, and sometimes another. Thus, *that* may be a pronoun, a conjunction, an adjective; *but* may be a preposition as well as a conjunction; and any word when spoken of as an object is a noun.

Exercise I.

Write out the first paragraph of "The King of the Golden River," arranging the words one below the other in columns down the page, and opposite each word indicate its part of speech. There are 234 words, of which 48 are nouns, 21 pronouns, 55 adjectives, 29 verbs, 27 adverbs, 82 prepositions, 22 conjunctions. A participle forming part of a compound verb should be reckoned a verb, but if it is used as an adjective it is to be reckoned an adjective. The possessive pronouns "its," "his," etc., are used in the adjective relation, but are reckoned pronouns. In the phrases "all below" and "country round," supply the implied words "that was" between the two words, showing the last word in each case to be an adverb. "Full" after "shone" should be considered a predicate adjective. In counting the words in each part of speech, check off with a pencil, so as to detect any omissions in counting. In case of doubt, consult the dictionary.

3

The Sentence

1. A Sentence

A sentence is a collection of words so chosen and arranged as completely to express a thought. Nouns may express ideas, but they do not represent a thought. The expression of a thought absolutely requires a verb united to a noun (or pronoun). The noun constitutes the *simple subject*, and the verb the *simple predicate* of the sentence. Any collection of words which does not contain both a subject and a predicate, expressed or implied, does not constitute a sentence or represent a thought. (Fragmentary phrases, if any special thought is attached to them, must be supposed to imply the lacking members.) The simple subject and the simple predicate may have modifiers, and together with these modifiers they constitute the *complete subject* and the *complete predicate.*

The following example will illustrate the fundamental and necessary division of every sentence into subject and predicate.

The Subject (noun)	***The Predicate (verb)***
The country *church*	*is* a square old building of wood.
It	*stands* upon a hill with a little churchyard in its rear where
one or two sickly *trees*	*keep* watch and ward over the vagrant sheep

that	*graze* among the graves.
Bramble *bushes*	*seem* to thrive on the bodies below.
	and
	there *is*
no *flower*	in the yard, save a few golden-rods
which	*flaunt* their gaudy, in-odorous colour under the lee of the northern wall.

2. Compound and Complex Sentences

Our first observation upon this is that each complete sentence seems to contain more than one subject and predicate. For instance, in the second sentence we have three subjects and three predicates, and also three in the next and last. We also observe, however, that each subject has its own definite predicate, and that the succeeding sets of subjects and predicates are connected with each other by conjunctions.

When the subjects and predicates are of equal importance, and are connected by conjunctions capable of connecting equals, we have a *compound* sentence; when one subject and predicate is subordinate to another, and is connected to it by a conjunction used to show subordinate relationship, we have a *complex* sentence.

3. Diagrams. Principal Subject etc.

In every sentence we must have a *principal subject* and a *principal predicate* to which all other words must be related.

In analysing any sentence, our first task should be to find the principal subject and the principal predicate and then trace out the chain of relationships of every other word to these. It is not difficult to make a picture, or diagram*, of these relationships, which will present the whole matter to the eye at a glance. We begin by drawing a straight line and dividing it distinctly in the middle, and then placing the subject noun or pronoun on the left and the predicate verb on the right, thus:

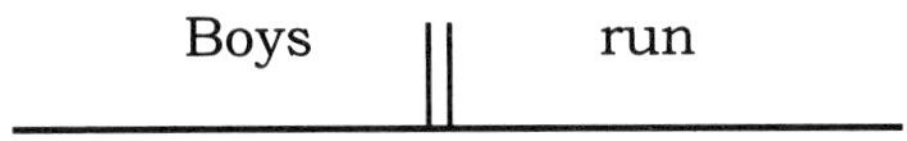

If we have any adjectives or adverbs, we may place them on slanting lines attached to the lines on which stand the words they modify, thus:

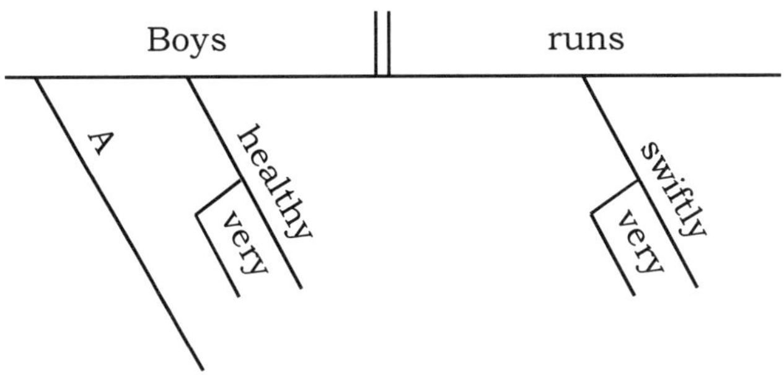

In this sentence *a* and *healthy* are adjectives modifying *boy*, the first *very* is an adverb modifying the adjective *healthy, swiftly* is an adverb modifying *runs*, and the second *very* an adverb modifying *swiftly*.

Phrases introduced by prepositions may be treated as follows:

*The diagram is liable to abuse, just as parsing is, but it helps us to comprehend that every word has a fixed relationship in the sentence. For a full exposition of the diagram see Reed and Kellogg's "Higher Lessons in English."

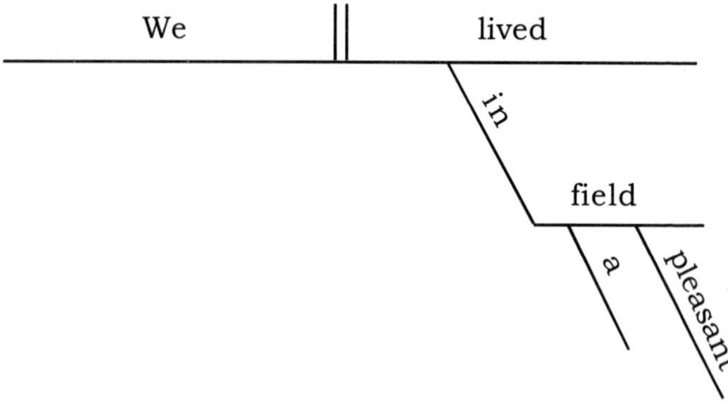

Subordinate sentences introduced by relative adverbs (or adverbial conjunctions) may be diagramed thus:

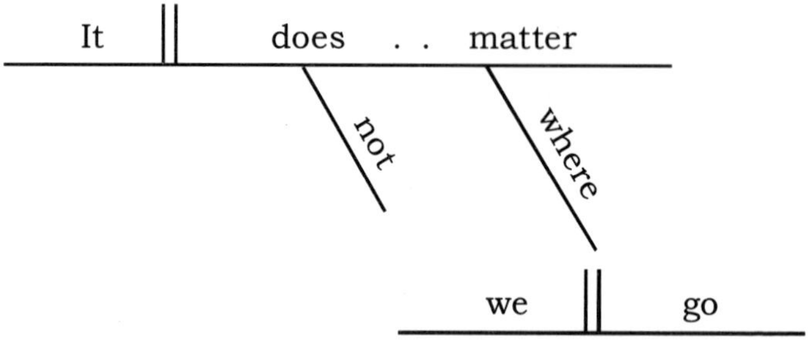

But subordinate sentences introduced by relative pronouns which have a necessary office in the subordinate sentence must be connected to the main sentence by a blank or dotted line, thus:

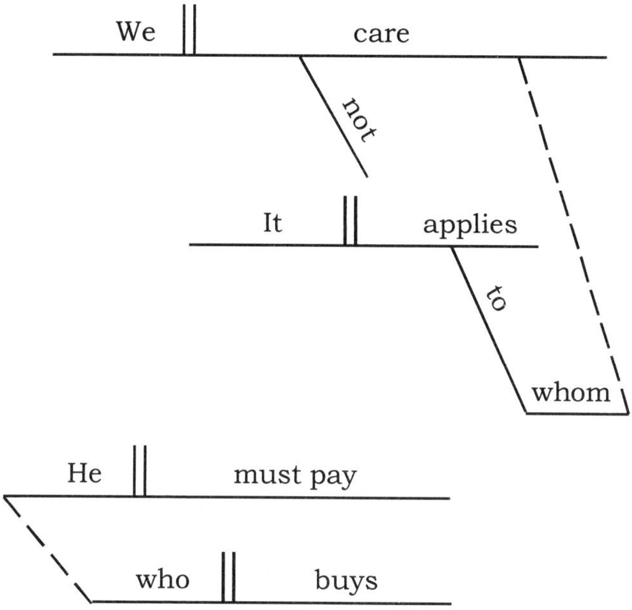

4. Two Laws

There are many other relationships besides those we have pictured; but these will illustrate the two most important laws in grammar, namely:

Law I. No collection of words expresses thought, and no sentence exists, unless a noun or pronoun (expressed or implied) unites with a verb (expressed or implied) to form a subject and a predicate.

Law II. Every word in a sentence must have a clear relationship, directly or through other words, to the principal simple subject or the principal simple predicate, that is, to the main noun or pronoun, or to the main verb.

5. Interjections

The only apparent exception to the last statement is the

interjection, which is a word that is as nearly independent as a word can be. Close logical analysis, however, will show, either that the interjection is in some way related to an adjoining sentence without which it would be devoid of meaning or significance; or it is a condensed sentence* in itself, distinctly implying a subject or a predicate or both. For instance, if we go about shouting "Fire! Fire! Fire!" we are simply condensing into a word some such full sentence as "There is a fire," or "Come and see the fire," or "Come and put out the fire." Implied words are frequent, and must always be supplied if we would understand grammatical relationships. Such interjections as "alas!" "oh!" "ah!" as a usual thing have no special meaning except in connection with some sentence, as in "Oh, I don't know." Grammarians have never found a name for this relationship, and in picturing such a sentence we set the interjection apart; but the relationship evidently exists, and we may remark in passing that it would have been just as well if the grammarians had failed to find names for some other relationships no more distinct than this.

Exercise II

Write out the first two paragraphs of "The King of the Golden River," placing all words pertaining to the subject of any sentence on the left hand side of the page, and all words pertaining to the predicate on the right hand side of the page, underscoring every simple subject and every simple predicate.

* Interjectory noises, such as grunts, squeals, etc., are the most primitive methods of expression. Animals usually have no other kind of speech (if speech this may be called.)

4

Cases of Nouns and Pronouns

1. Abstract Noun

Nouns, we have learned, are the names of things. An idea, a thought, an act may also have a name, which is a noun (called *abstract*). Several forms of the verb and verbal phrases are also used as nouns, as in "*Doing* is better than *waiting*," "*To be cautious* is a necessity in speculation," and "*Growing old* should not make a man sour."

2. Subjective and Objective Cases

We have seen nouns as subjects of verbs, the starting-points of sentences. They may also be objects of verbs or prepositions. A preposition must have a noun as object, since the sole office of prepositions is to introduce nouns, or pronouns. Unless a word has such an object, it is not a preposition. Active verbs also take a noun as object when they are of such a nature that they express action which passes over to an object. Thus when we say "He killed a man," the word *man* is an object noun, since the action of the subject as expressed in the verb passes over and takes effect on the object *man*.

Subject nouns are said to be in the *sudjective* or nominative case, and object nouns are said to be in the objective case.

3. Predicate Nominative

Not all nouns that follow verbs are in the objective case. All nouns following the verb to be or its parts (*am, is, are, was, were, would be, have teen, might be*) are in the subjective or nominative case, and are called *predicate nominatives,* because the verb to he merely asserts that the subject is the same as the noun in the predicate. Thus in "John is a man," *man* is precisely the same as the subject and the verb *is* merely asserts this sameness. So also in the sentence "John will become a man," *man* and *John* are equivalent, or are in the process of becoming so. There is no action which passes over to an object. Of course in the sentence, "He killed himself," *he* and *himself* are the same, but in this case the man is the object of his own act.

4. Case Forms of Pronouns. Errors

Nouns in English have the same form, whether they are in the nominative or in the objective case. But pronouns, the words which stand for nouns and are used so very frequently, have in many cases different forms for the nominative and objective cases, as follows:

Nominative	***Objective***
I	me
we	us
he	him
she	her
they	them
who	whom

Therefore we should always say "It is I," not "It is me," "It is he, she, they, or we," not "It is him, her, them, or us," as we often hear people say. Also, remembering that the object of a preposition is always in the objective case, we will say "between you and me," not "between you and I," "It can be done by you and me," not "It can be done by you and I." We would not say "between I and the fence-post," nor "It is being done by I and somebody else." These sound absurd. It is quite as absurd to say "between you or the fence-post and I."

5. Verbs Which Take Predicate Nominative

The verbs followed by the nominative case are very few, but they are so common that they occur as often, probably, as all other verbs put together. They are chiefly *to be* (*is, am, was, were, would be, have been,* etc.), *to become, to appear,* and *to seem.* There is no action expressed by these verbs, only a state or condition of existence.

6. Possessive Case

Nouns and pronouns also have a third case, the possessive, indicated in nouns by the apostrophe and s or the apostrophe alone. The possessive case has precisely the logical relation in a sentence that an adjective has, that is, it is a direct modifier of a noun, and is used in no other way, though often the noun it modifies is implied. Like a noun, however, it is modified by adjectives, not by adverbs. The case offers no special difficulty, it is usually interchangeable with a prepositional phrase containing of.

> **Note.** Nouns in the singular regularly form the possessive case by adding an apostrophe and *s,* as *man's, John's, Dickens's.* Some writers omit the *s*

when the singular form itself ends with *s* or an equivalent sound, and write *Dickens', conscience'*, etc.; but the best usage is always to write the *s* after the apostrophe even if it cannot be pronounced. Plural nouns ending in *s* take merely the apostrophe to indicate the possessive case, as *cows', hens'*, etc. If, however, the plural form does not end in *s*, the apostrophe must be followed by *s*, as in *men's, children's*, etc. Pronouns never take an apostrophe to indicate the possessive case. We write *its, his*, etc. *It's* is a contraction for *it* is and must not be confused with the possessive case of *it*.

7. Apposition

When one noun follows another as an alternative name for the same thing, or to explain the preceding noun, it is said to be in *apposition* with the noun it explains; and as nouns which are in every way equivalent should agree in case, it is an established rule that a noun in apposition with another noun agrees in case with that other noun; and the same rule applies to pronouns, since they take the place of nouns. Thus: "William, conqueror of England, became king." *Conqueror* is equivalent to *William* and is added by way of explanation.

8. To Avoid Awakwardness with Possessive

The application of this rule to the possessive case is very awkward, however, and is always to be avoided. In some cases in which the explanatory noun is absolutely required, the possessive sign is omitted from one or the other of the pair; and in some cases the whole phrase is treated as a compound word and the sign of the possessive put at the end of the whole. The same rule applies when the possessive has modifiers of any other kind.

Thus we may say, "I called at Smith's, the bookseller." This is so evident a violation of a well known rule that it should be avoided as much as possible, though the best usage justifies it. We seem to be more logical when we say, "I called at Smith the bookseller's." The latter is the form to be preferred in all such expressions as "William the Conqueror's," "The captain of the guard's house," etc.

9. Diagraming Predicate Complements

We have seen that a verb may be followed by an object noun or by a "predicate nominative"—a noun in the nominative case which means the same as the subject of the verb. The verb may also assert a quality or characteristic of the subject by the use of an adjective in the predicate which really qualifies the subject, as when we say "He is good" we assert the quality of goodness as belonging to the subject *he.*

These *predicate complements,* as they are called, may be pictured as follows :

A noun as the direct object of a verb, as in "He killed the man"—

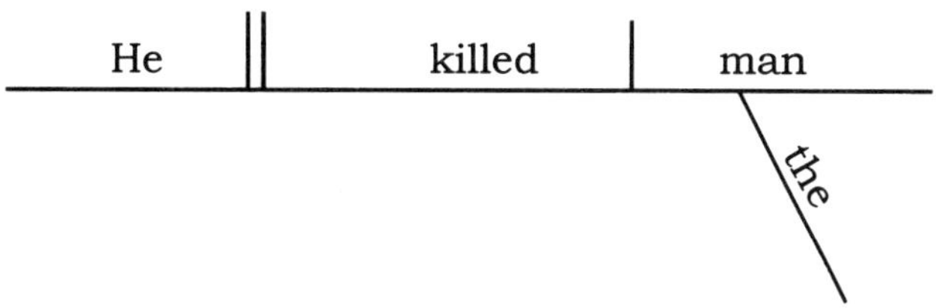

A noun as predicative nominative, as in "His name was John"—

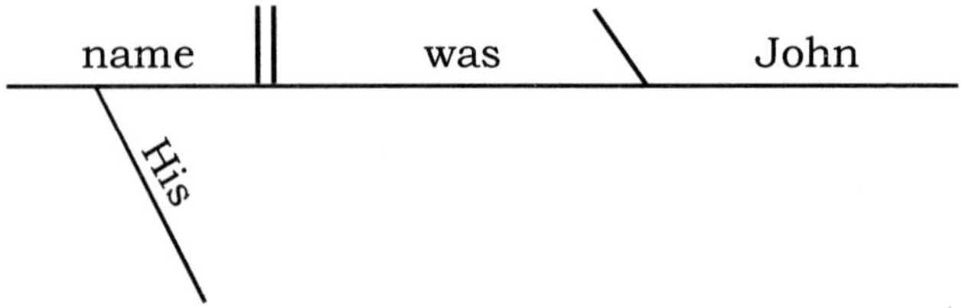

An adjective expressing a quality asserted of the subject, as in "That story is excellent"—

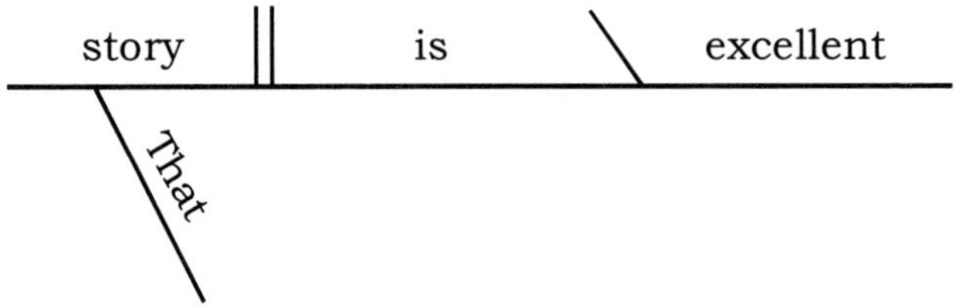

Sameness may be asserted between two objects of an active verb, as in "We named him John." Which may be pictured thus:

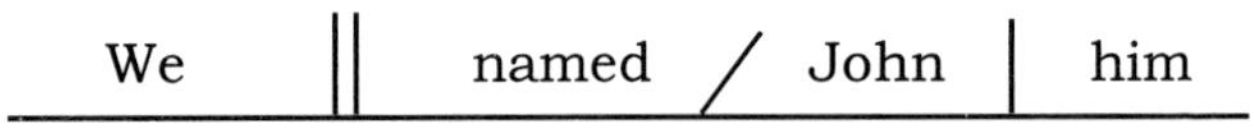

(In this case *John* is placed before *him*, though *him* is more closely related to the verb, in order that the slanting line before *John* may clearly indicate that the word is to be connected with *him*. If *John* followed *him*, preceded by a slanting line, it might seem to refer back to the subject, *we*.)

In the same way an active verb may assert a quality of its object, as in "The medicine will make you sick," which may be diagramed as follows:

These secondary objects and qualifiers are spoken of as objective nouns and adjectives, or objective complements.

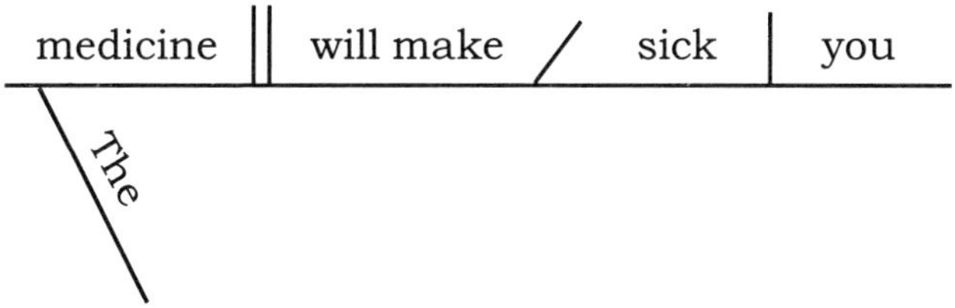

Exercise III

Arrange the words in the second paragraph of "The King of the Golden River" in columns, and opposite each indicate the part of speech, and also case of nouns and pronouns. There are a total of 267 Words, of which 38 are nouns or pronouns in the nominative or subjective case, 52 in the objective case, 4 in the possessive; 47 verbs, 48 adjectives, 27 adverbs, 31 prepositions, and 25 conjunctions. Observe that in several cases participles are used as nouns in the objective case and also govern other nouns in the objective. Supply words when needed to show the construction, as in "had given so much (money) as a penny (is)" etc. "Treasure Valley" is properly one name, but we treat it as adjective and noun, as we do "Black Brothers." "Yet" may be a conjunction as well as an adverb.

Complete these sentences: "It is (I—me)", "Between you and (I—me), I do not like him;" "Such a man as (he—him), should do better;" "The thief was—(I—me) ;" "Let us (you and I—me) see that the wrong is righted;" : Let "he—him) who under stands the case best be our spokesman."

5

The Verb
(Auxiliaries; Person and Number)

1. Auxiliary Verbs

The verb offers far more complications than any other part of speech. In the first place, it often consists of more than one word. There are a number of verbs known as auxiliary verbs, some of which are used only as auxiliaries, and some of which may also appear as independent verbs.

The three most important auxiliaries are to be, to have, and to do, all of which may also be used independently. *To be* is the most irregular verb in the English language, and has many forms apparently utterly unlike, as *am, is, are, was, were,* as well as *be* and *been* and some antiquated forms like *beest,* etc.

2. *To be* as Auxiliary; Passive and Progressive Voices

The verb *to be* indicates existence in the simplest and most direct way in which it can be indicated, and has the force of asserting without asserting anything in particular. The particular character of the assertion is to be looked for in the words which follow. This verb is used to indicate what is called the *passive voice*, or a form of assertion in which the subject bears everything but actually does nothing. *For example,* "I am wounded," "You were loved," "He is ruined," are illustration of the passive voice, in which parts of the verb *to be* appear as auxiliaries to the verb forms which contain the real significance.

To be is also used to indicate what is called the *progressive* form of the verb, which asserts the action or state as continuing at the time indicated by the tense of the verb, as "I am going there now," "He was reading a book," "You were thinking about it at that time."

3. *To have* as Auxiliary; Perfect Tenses

The verb *to have* is used as an auxiliary, to indicate a peculiar state of completeness in the action at a given time, as "I have already done it" (at the present time), "I had told him all about it" (at the past time to which I refer), etc. The forms in which *to have* and its parts occur as auxiliaries are spoken of as the *perfect tenses,* since they assert the action as being *perfect* or completed at a certain time, either past, present or future.

4. *To do* as Auxiliary

The verb *to do* is used as an auxiliary to give peculiar emphasis to an assertion, as in "I do love you," in asking question without emphasis, as "Do you see it?" and with negatives, as "She did not come to the party."

5. *Shall* and *Will* Form Future Tense

Shall and will are the two words regularly used to indicate action or state of being at, a future time, as in "I shall go there tomorrow," "Will you do as I ask you?" *Shall* is regularly used with the first person (I and we), *will* with other persons; but there are many variations from this rule which we shall consider later.

6. *Should* and *Would*

Should and would are apparently past tenses of *shall* and *will*, but as auxiliaries they indicate conditional action or state of being, as in "Would you have done it, had I requested it?" These words are usually found in constructions which contain or imply a subordinate sentence introduced by *if* or some similar word. In the example above, "had I requested it" is equivalent to "if I had requested it."

7. *May, Can, Must, Could, Might, Let;* Potential Mode; Indicative

Can, may, and their corresponding past forms could and might, are used to indicate possibility of some kind, and indicate, with *should* and *would*, what is called the *potential* mode. Simple assertion constitutes the *indicative* mode. *Must* and *let* may also be ranked as auxiliaries.

8. Tense Defined

All verbs indicate the time of the action or state of being as present, past, or future, and accordingly are said to be in the present, past, or future *tense* (tense meaning time). Thus "I am here" is in the present tense, "I went to town yesterday" is in the past tense, "I shall be hungry at dinner time" is in the future tense. The past and present tenses are regularly indicated by different forms of the verb, *ed* being added to the present to indicate the past, as in "I love you" (present) and "I loved you once" (past). *Loving* is a present form, as *loved* is past.

9. Number and Person

The English verb ordinarily has but one other irregularity or variation, and that is used to indicate the third person singular of the indicative mode. To understand that, we must know the meaning of *person* and *number.*

Number—All nouns or pronouns are either plural or singular in number. *I, he, she, it cow, horse, cat, dog,* are all singular because they refer to only one object; but *we, they, cows, horses, cats, dogs,* are plural, because each refers to more than one object.

Person—The person speaking is the first person (I or we), the person spoken to is the second person (you, thou), while the person spoken of is the third person (he, she, it, they, these, etc.)

> **Rule**—The verb must agree with its subject in person and number. In English the form of the verb is usually the same for all persons and numbers, except the third person singular of the present indicative, and the forms derived from it. The only exception is found in the case of the irregular verb *to be* and the forms used with the now antiquated pronoun *thou.*

Thus we conjugate the verb *to be*:

Present tense		***Past tense***	
I do	We do	I did	We did
You do	You do	You did	You did
He does	They do	He did	They did

The only irregular form that we find here is "he does." Instead of *he* we may substitute any singular subject in the third person, that is, any noun or pronoun (not *I, we,* or *you*), and say "A man does," "Helen does," "It does," "One does." Our instincts are sufficiently good guides for most cases. We would not say* "The babies does all

* But some people say, "He don't do it" for "He doesn't do it," though they would not say "He do not do it."

they likes," nor "John do many hard jobs." But there are many words and combinations which do not show clearly on their face whether they are singular or plural. "John and' Helen" would be followed by a plural form of the verb, because the two taken together are used as the subject; but "John or Helen" would be followed by the singular form of the verb, because we are thinking of either one, but not of both the same time.

10. *Every* Indicates the Singular

"All of us" is plural, evidently, but "Every one of us," which means practically the same thing, as it would seem, is singular, because "Every one of us" means all of us taken one at time, and the form of the verb must be singular. So also "Every man and woman" is singular, because though *man* and *woman* taken together are plural, the *every* indicates that we take only one man or one woman at a time; hence the verb which follows must be singular.

11. *None* Either Plural or Singular

Some modern grammarians contend that the word *none* is singular because it is evidently derived by a contraction of *no one,* but the best authorities hold that *none* may be either singular or plural, and a phrase such as "None of the men remains or remain in the room" may mean that the very last man is gone, or that the last group of men is gone. If we are thinking of the last man, *none* is singular, but if we mean the last group of men, *none* is plural. So some gram- marians contend that "a number of men" is always singular, because there is but one "number." But in such a sentence as "A number of us are going to town" it is better to regard "a number" as a plural form, in analogy with the plural form "a few of us," which every one admits to be plural. If, however, we are thinking of a definite number, even when we use the general phrases "a large number," or "a small number," a singular verb should be used.

12. Collective Nouns

Another class of nouns which gives difficulty is the so called collective nouns, such as *people, crowd, army, multitude,* etc. These words are followed either by the singular or by the plural form of the verb, according as we think of the collection as a single body, or a number of individuals in a group. Thus we should certainly say, "The army is encamped on the plain," and equally clearly we would say, "People say it is not true."

13. Logical Principle Governing Singular or Plural Verb

The form of the verb should show the nature of the subject. The correct form is the one that expresses our thought with logical exactness. If we use the singular form of the verb it should mean that we wish to refer to the subject as a single object, but if we use the plural form it should show that we are thinking of all the various single objects that go to make up the whole, and that we are thinking of each as acting alone.

Nothing demonstrates better than this that grammar is a matter of logical relationships of words and phrases used to express ideas. Violations of grammar arise more from carelessness than from anything else, and the study of correct language should be, not a study of rules, but a study of the exact meaning of words, and their exact logical relations to other words in the accurate expression of ideas.

Exercise IV

Form sentences using each of the following words or groups of words in the subject, with a verb in the present tense (singular or plural). If a word has more than one meaning or use, form a sentence for each such meaning or use : People, he and I, I and he, he or I, I or he, either, one, none, number, army, crowd, every, each, some, all, much, you or he, I and they, several, few (a few), many (many a), plenty.

6

The Verb
(Participles and Infinitives)

1. The Participle and the Infinitive

Many writers have ranked the *participle* as a separate part of speech. It is in reality a sort of hybrid, half verb and half adjective, and may become a noun. The *infinitive* is also a curious form of the verb, for it may often be used as a noun and is interchangeable to some extent with the present participle.

There are two forms of the participle, the present, ending in *ing,* and the past ending regularly in *ed* (but also being formed with other endings). The infinitive is indicated by the preposition *to*, which often wholly loses its character as a preposition in introducing one word to another, and serves merely as the sign of the infinitive mode of the verb. In this case the infinitive is to be regarded as a verbal noun.

Examples: Present participle as simple adjective—"The *boxing* parson preached today."

Past participle as simple adjective "The *learned* doctor delivered the address;" "The *past* year shows a good report;" "The work *begun* is a credit to the town."

Present participle as noun "By *signing* your name here you will secure your rights;" "I like *riding.*"

Infinitive as noun—"*To be* good is *to be* wise."

2. Office of the Infinitive

The chief office of the infinitive is simply to complete the meaning of other verbs, as when we say, "I like *to ride*;" "He is going *to do* it;" etc. Here the assertion that Is made in regard to the subject is not complete until the infinitive is added, and we may look on the first verb as more or less of an auxiliary. In fact, "He will do it" and "He is going to do it" are very much alike, and grammarians look on the *do* after *will* as an infinitive with the sign (*to*) omitted. However, in all cases in which the to is expressed we are accustomed to treat the infinitive as separate from the verb, and picture it in our diagrams as an ordinary prepositional phrase, thus:

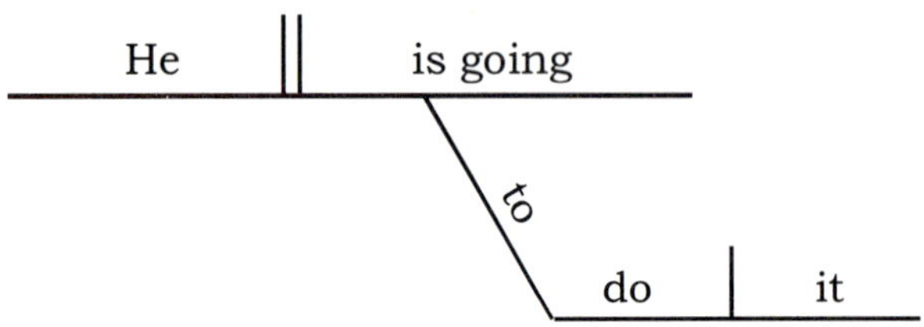

3. Subject of Ifinitive in Objective Case; Infinitive as Noun

But the infinitive may have a subject of its own, which will always be in the objective case. In such a relation the *to* is commonly omitted as in "I shall make him do it," which may he diagramed thus:

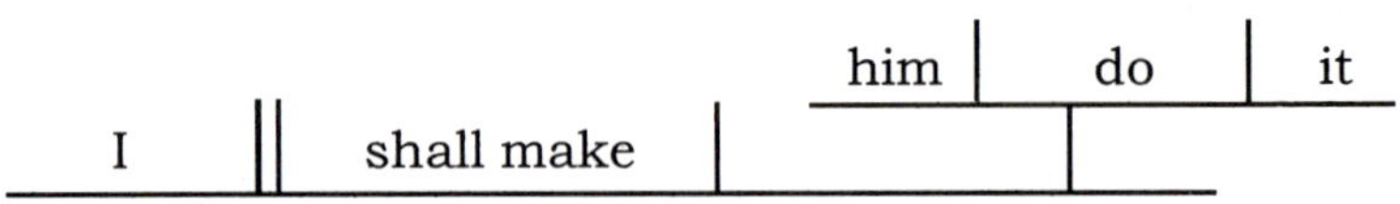

Here the whole phrase, "him do it," may he regarded as taking the place of a noun and forming the object of *shall make*, though it would not be altogether improper to place it below and connect it with *shall make* by a dotted line, after the manner of a subordinate sentence.

In such cases as "To be good is to be wise," the *to* merely introduces the verbal phrases which serve as nouns, and we may picture the sentence as follows:

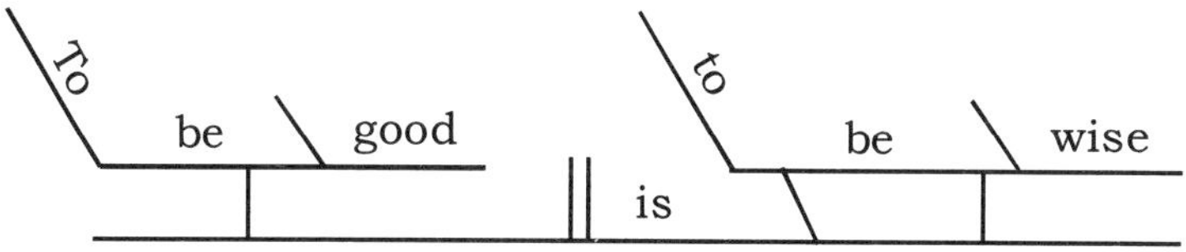

4. Characteristics of Infinitive

Fully to explain such a sentence grammatically and logically, however, we must reflect that a personal subject is implied, such as "any one," "any person." The adjective *good* and the adjective *wise* really qualify this indefinite implied personality.

We see, however, that while acting as a verbal noun, an infinitive may exercise all the qualities of a verb in taking predicate modifiers, either nouns or adjectives; and it may also be modified by adverbs.

5. The Participle; Diagram

The participles may also exercise the functions of verbs in the same way, as in the sentence, "I found him rapidly *writing* letters," which we may picture as follows:

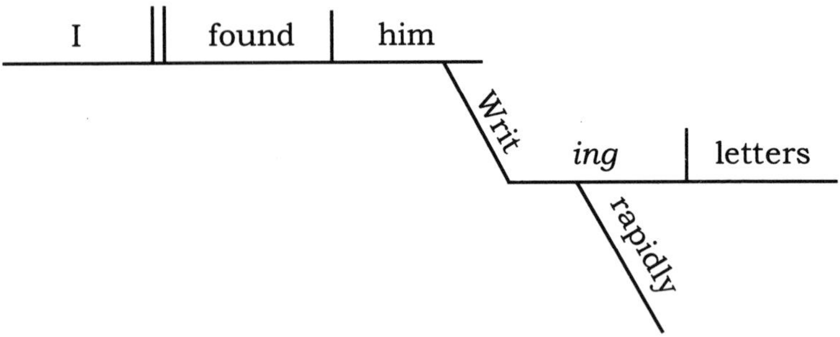

Or, if we wish to show that the real object of *found* is not so much *him* as the action expressed in *writing*, we may put the whole phrase on a bracket, slightly breaking the line on which *writing* stands to show its double character of adjective and verb:

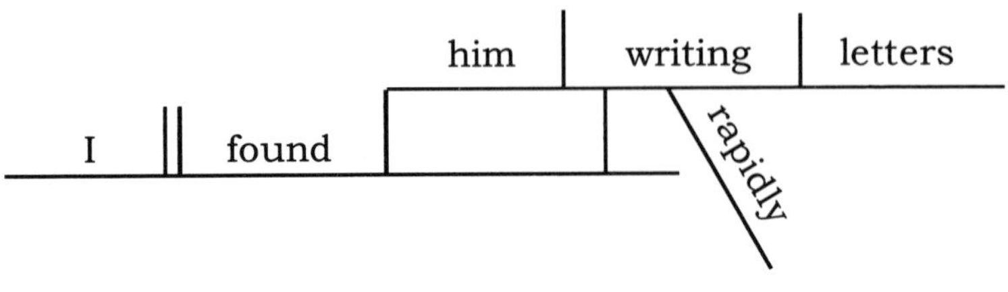

6. Infinitives must have Subject

We have already seen that the subject noun and the assertive verb are both indispensable to any expression of thought. We may realize how far-reaching and important this principle is when we know that every verb, whatever its form, even the participle and the infinitive in so far as they exercise any of the functions of verbs, must have subjects of some kind, expressed or implied. If an infinitive is used to complete a verb, we look back through the auxiliary verb and find the real subject of the action or state expressed by the infinitive, in the subject of the sentence. Thus in the sentence, "I should like to do it," the logical subject of the act of doing is *I*. If we say, "I should like to have him do it," the subject of *have* is logically *I*, and of *do, him*.

7. Participles must have Subject which is Clearly Traced

The same is true of participles. Thus in the sentence, "While sitting on my doorstep yesterday, I caught sight of the most beautiful butterfly in the world." Here *sitting* is a participle evidently modifying the subject of the sentence, *I*. If we change the form of the sentence so as to make it read, "While sitting on my doorstep yesterday, my notice was attracted to the most beautiful butterfly in the world," we perceive that the real subject of the participle verb *sitting* is hard to find. It is perhaps implied in the possessive *my*, but it would be out of the question, grammatically, to attach *sitting* to *my*. If we should say, "While sitting on the doorstep yesterday, the most beautiful butterfly in the world attracted my notice," we would seem to imply that the butterfly was sitting, which is of course absurd. The sentences are manifestly imperfect from a logical point of view.

8. Errors in Use of Participles and Infinitives

Even if the sentence is so constructed that it is not difficult to account for all the members, still if the subject of the infinitive or participle is obscured, the sentence is imperfect. Thus if we say, "To relieve him of all responsibility, he was given a written statement by the members of the firm," *To relieve* is evidently a simple qualifier of the verb *was given*, but whatever act was performed in relieving was not by he, the subject of *was given*, but by *members*, which appears in a subordinate phrase. The sentence is logically imperfect, though every word of it can be parsed. The same is true of the sentence, "By doing so, the matter will be cleared up by him."

9. Nominative Absolute

There are various ways of legitimately relieving this situation, which we will now explain.

First, there is what is called the *nominative absolute.* A participle may stand as an independent verb with a nominative case as its subject, though always in a dependent relation to some principal sentence, as in "The wind blowing furiously, the boat was overset;" "He knowing that, I had no choice but to act as I did." *The wind* is subject of the participle *blowing*, and *He* is the subject of the independent participle *knowing*. Both *he* and *wind* are spoken of as independent nominatives, though they are no more independent than any other subjects of verbs. It would be more just to speak of the participles as independent in their use, for here they perform the offices of an ordinary verb even to having a separate subject in the nominative case. This use is not favored by the best critics or writers, and evidently grew up because the instincts of the mind sought to supply a suitable subject for the participle when no implied subject was in sight. This is a bungling method of relieving the logical incompleteness of such sentences as we discussed in the preceding paragraph.

10. Subject of Participle Implied in Possessive

The subject of the participle may be implied in a possessive, as in the sentence, "By his doing that, the situation was relieved." Here the character of the participle as noun is emphasized by the presence of a possessive used as a simple adjective modifier; but the subject of the assertive power in the participle is clear.

11. Participle does not take Objective Case as Subject

The participle, unlike the infinitive, never takes the objective case as its subject if this can be avoided. So we should say, "I could not prevent his doing it," rather than "I could not prevent him doing it," though we may say correctly enough, "I could not prevent him from doing it."

12. Implied Subjects for Participles and Infinitives

We have already given an example of an indefinite subject's being implied when an infinitive is used in a general sense. The subject of the participle may be implied in the same way when it is general or indefinite, as in "Speaking of the President, what did you think of his manifesto?" "Granting all that, still how do you account for the strange circumstances?" *Granting* and *speaking* are evidently independent with such subjects as *we, you,* etc., implied. Unless the subject is *clearly* implied, this method is objectionable.

Exercise V

Construct logical sentences containing the following participial clauses (three forms for each): "Referring to your letter of yesterday;" "Weighing up the sugar, shortage;" "Having dressed the leather on both sides;" "Suggesting all sorts of conditions;" "Granting that we were wrong."

Carefully trace the subject of each participle and indicate it by underscoring.

Look over any accessible file of correspondence and find three examples of participles not logically connected to their subjects (actual cases).

7

The Verb
(Tense, Mode, Irregular Forms)

1. Names of Tenses

We have already seen that verbs are capable of expressing present, past, and future time; and, by the use of the auxiliary *have*, completeness of an act at a given time present, past, or future may be indicated. Time as expressed by verbs is known as tense.

In simple sentences, tense offers few difficulties. The following illustrations will serve to explain names of tenses sometimes used:

Present Tense

The house *stands* on a hill.

We *have* our commands.

I *am doing* the work now.

It *makes* no difference to you whether I *do* it or not.

Past Tense*

I *went* there yesterday.

I *loved* her, but she *did* not *love* me.

They *gave* me all I asked.

* Also called the "imperfect" to distinguish it from the past tense of the participle.

We *began* to eat at three o'clock.

He *spit* as If he had tasted poison.

Future Tense

We *shall* be there.

They *will see* what *will be* the result.

You *shall do it,* whether you wish to or not.

Perfect, or Present Perfect, Tense

I *have done* what I could.

He *has been* to town.

He *has* not *come* yet.

I *have* already *done* so.

Pluperfect or Past Perfect, Tense

They *had* not *arrived* when I was there yesterday.

You *had gone* before I got there.

Future Perfect Tense

When I have finished, I *shall have proved* my case completely.

In that case, I *shall have been defeated.*

Participles and infinitives also express time to some extent, as:

Present —*going, to go.*

Past—*gone,* (the infinitive has no simple past tense.)

Present perfect—*having gone, to have gone.*

Past perfect—(wanting.)

Future—wanting.

2. Errors in Tenses

Error sometimes occurs in using or failing to use the perfect tenses when required by the use of adverbs which imply completeness at a fixed time. We should say, "I have done it already," not "I did it already," and I have not yet done it," not "I did not do it yet." The tense and the adverb indicating time must be consistent. Likewise, do not say "I have done it yesterday."

3. Sequence of Tenses in Subordinate Sentences

The chief difficulty arises in the choosing of tenses in subordinate sentences or phrases. We should be guided by the great principle of *sequence of tenses*, namely.

Verbs in subordinate sentences must be governed by the tense of the principal verb.

We may test and correct the application of this principle by inquiring whether the tenses we use express exactly the relations of time that accord with the facts in the case.

Examples: I *see* the new building every time I *go* to town.

I *saw* it when I *was* there.

He *said* he *would* do it.

He *says* he *will* do it.

To *have done* otherwise *would have been* wrong.

We may not say, "I wish *to have done* it," for it is impossible to "wish for" that which is past. It is more proper to say I should have liked to do it." than "I should like to have done it," since it is a little awkward for our liking to go backward, though even this is not impossible.

We would not say "The Lord hath given and the Lord hath taken away," since the giving took place before the taking away, and the meaning must be expressed by saying, 'The Lord *gave* and the Lord hath taken away."

"John will earn his wages when his service is complete," is illogical and should be expressed, "John *will have earned* his wages when his service shall be complete."

"After we visited New York, we returned, content and thankful, to our retired and peaceful habitation," should obviously be, "After we *had* visited New York," etc.

But we may say, "After we visited New York, we went to Baltimore," since the time is continuous.

"In the little conversation I had with him, he appeared to have been a man of letters," requires "to be" in the place of "to have been."

"We have done no more than it was our duty to have done," should be either, "We have done no more than it was our duty to do," or "We did no more than it was our duty to do," according to the meaning intended by the writer.

When the statement in the subordinate sentence is of universal application, whether the time be past, present, or future, we must use the present tense. "The doctor, in his lecture, said that fever always produced thirst," should be, "The doctor, in his lecture, said that fever always *produces* thirst"

"I will attend to the business as soon as I have finished my letter," is correct, though "I will attend to the business as soon as I *shall* have finished my letter," is logically more complete.

4. Mode

The different modes have already been defined. The *indicative* mode, expressing simple, direct assertion, offers no difficulties; the *potential* mode consists in little more than the use of the potential auxiliaries, *may, can, would, should, could, might, must;* the *infinitive* mode has been discussed; the imperative mode is peculiar in that it is confined to the second person, or person spoken to, and usually omits the subject. Examples of the imperative mode are—"*Do* this," "Never do it," "*Hear* what I say," etc. Perhaps "let" may be looked on as an auxiliary for the imperative mode, permitting reference to other persons than the second, as in "Let me do it," "Let her see you for a moment," etc. In full these forms become, "(Do you) let me (to) do it," "(Do you) let her (to) see you for a moment," etc. Or the *do* may be omitted.

5. Subjunctive Mode

The mode which really gives trouble is the *subjunctive.* It differs from the simple indicative in not forming its third person singular by the addition of *e* or *es,* and we say, "If he do it, it will be of the greatest benefit." The irregular verb *to be,* uses the form *be* throughout the present tense of the subjunctive mode, as "If I be, if you be, if he be, if we be, if you be, if they be;" and *were* throughout the past tense of the subjunctive, as "If I were, if you were, if he were, if we were, if you were, if they were."

It is the office of the subjunctive mode to indicate supposed cases as opposed to cases of fact. Thus, we say, "If he was (as a matter of fact) there, he saw Anna on the "'stage;" but, "If he were here (as he is not), he would see Anna on the stage." Suet phrases as "as it were" are typical of the subjunctive mode, and other conjunctions than *if* may be used with it. Examples: "Unless he do it, it will go hard with him;" "Though he be a giant, he will have to succumb to such oratory;" "Though he slay me, yet will I trust in him;" "Whether he improve or not, it matters little;" "Except ye repent, ye shall surely die;" "Reprove not a scorner, lest he hate thee."

The subjunctive mode is used to express *wishes*, which are very similar to suppositions.

It will be noted that the subjunctive mode often indicates that which is in the future, even with the present and past tenses, since what is really accomplished, either past or present, is not a subject for supposition, as a rule. Perhaps this accounts for the omission of s or es from the third person of the present tense, *will* having been omitted, as in "If he (will) do it, it will be of the greatest benefit."

There is a growing tendency to disregard the subjunctive mode as much as possible, and some writers even deny that it exists at all in the English language. The crude speaker will seldom have occasion to use it, except in idiomatic and well established phrases, such as "as it were," but the precise thinker and reasoner will find the subjunctive mode of the utmost utility, and a means of expressing nice distinctions that are otherwise almost impossible of expression.

6. Irregularities of Form

We have called attention to the various irregularities of the verb *to be* in the different modes and tenses. Besides this verb, there are over one hundred and seventy other verbs that are classed as irregular; but their irregularity extends only to the past tense and the past participle, and forms derived from them.

The following illustrations will serve to indicate this class:

Present	***Past***	***Past participle***
arise	arose	arisen
build	built	built
bite	bit	bitten
spit	spit	spit
begin	began	begun
put	put	put
catch	caught	caught
teach	taught	taught
drink	drank	drunk or drank

The chief difficulty with such verbs arises from confusing the past tense with the past participle. Many people will say "I done it," and some even "I have did it."

7. Example of Use of Irregular Verbs; Errors

There are not many of the irregular verbs that offer difficulty. Before considering them, let us see just when and where we should use the past tense, and where and when the past participle.

The auxiliaries *to be* and *to have* are followed by the past participle in forming the various modes, tenses, etc., of the verb, but all the other auxiliaries are followed by the present form (the present infinitive without the *to*). We can make no error if we always place the participle after forms of *be* and *have*, but use the past form when *be* and *have* are wanting in regular sentences. The following illustrations will serve to enforce this observation. In each case the past tense of the verb is used before the participial form:

He *bore* the colors before the regiment;

but He *had borne* his comrades from the field.

He *bade* me tell you he was ready to see you;

but He *was bidden* to apologize.

He *came* up here to see you;

but He *had come* up here to see you.

We all *did* our best;

but Everything *was done* that could be done.

We *forgot* to ask his opinion;

but The incident was *forgotten* an hour later.

He *laid* the book on the table;

When he came in he was so tired he *lay* down to rest;

but She *had lain* down to rest;

The towel *had been laid* away and I could not find it.

Note—Distinguish the parts of these two entirely different verbs carefully. They are often confused.

We *saw* the parade;

but She lives merely to see and to *be seen.*

The wind *shook* the tree till it trembled;

but The tree *was shaken* till it fell.

The sun *shone* in at the window;

and The sun *had shone* brightly all day;

but He *showed* us the jewels which *had* before *been shown* to the prince.

Note—that here we have two entirely different verbs.)

The student may make similar examples for himself correctly using the following:

Present	***Past***	***Past participle***
speak	spoke	spoken
steal	stole	stolen
swear	swore	sworn
take	took	taken
wear	wore	worn
write	wrote	written

The common error in the use of the above may be readily seen by placing the past participle where the past tense form should be found. The student will do well to read the above sentences with the past participle in place of the past tense as, "He *come* up here to see you;" and if the past participle is not liable to such misuse, replace the participle by the past tense, as "He *had* bore his comrade from the field." Such an experiment once tried will doubtless put the student on his guard. It is better that the student should try the experiment for himself without writing out the sentence than that his teacher should offer him incorrect examples on which his mind may dwell too long; study should be concentrated on the *correct* usage.

There is a class of Irregular verbs In which the principle vowel may be u or a, as "Drink, drank, drunk or drank." Usage differs a little on these, but sometimes both forms are right. In the example given above some use "drank" in both past tense and past participle, to avoid con fusion with the adjective "drunk," but "drunk" in the past tense is obsolete. The following table will show the preferred usage with most of these verbs:

drink	drank	drunk
sing	sang or sung	sung
sink	sank or sunk	sunk
spring	sprang or sprung	sprung
swim	swam or swum	swum

"Read" has the same form in all three parts, but the two past forms are pronounced with the short sound of e. "Eat" is peculiar in having "eat, ate, eaten," and it is incorrect to say, "He has eat it all up," and "When he eat his breakfast yesterday morning, etc." is an obsolete use of "eat."

Those who are in the habit of reading standard literature with some thought for the values of words will seldom err in the use of the irregular verbs. "I done it" seems to be the chief survival of barbarism among persons of more or less education. "I seen" Is a sign of gross ignorance.

Exercise VI

Supply the proper verb in the following : "She (sets—sits) by the window enjoying the scene that (lays—lies) before her;" "The sun (sets—sits);" "The hen (sets-sits);" "If you feel ill, (lay-lie) down;" "Your coat (sits—sets) well;" "If It (rain— rains), I cannot go;" "If John (were—was) here fee would enjoy this sunset;" "If you (drank—drunk) all that water, no wonder you are sick;" "I cannot; (learn—teach) him the knack;" "(Can—may) I speak to you?" He (hadn't ought—ought not) to do it;" "He oughtn't to do it, (had—) he?" "If it (is—be) a fine day tomorrow, I will walk with you;" "If Jack (be—is) in town, he will call;" "If Jack (were—was) in town, he would call;" "I wish it (were—was) in my power to help you;" "If he (be—is) discreet, all will go well with him;" "If ye (be are) men, fight:" "We hoped (to have seen—see) you;" "You ought to have helped Susan (to do—to have done) it;" "Had you known how short life (was—is), you would have made better use of your time;" "He (need—needs) not leave his office;" "He (dare—dares) not do it."

Form sentences using each of these words correctly: Sit, set, sat, lay, lie, laid, lain, come, drunk, bid, bade, sung, run, learn, teach—one sentence for each verb form which each word may represent.

8

Pronouns, Adjectives and Other Parts of Speech

1. Use of Pronouns

As we know, a pronoun is a word which stands for a noun; and it requires little reflection to show how very important it is that we should know clearly for what noun each pronoun stands.

Every pronoun must agree with its antecedent in every respect, and the relationship must be easily and clearly traced, without danger of confusion.

We usually have no special difficulty in knowing to whom the first and second persons refer, for one is the person speaking, and the other the person spoken to, the two chief actors in every dialogue, the rhetorical essentials in every written or spoken discourse.

Pronouns of the third person, however, are used so numerously, and even in the same sentence refer so variously to different persons and objects, that confusion is not only easy, but inevitable unless the greater care is taken. Here is a sentence from Lane's translation of the "Arabian Nights": "Aladdin was so frightened at what he saw that he would have run away; but as *he* was to be serviceable to the magician, *he* caught hold of *him*, scolded *him*, and gave *him* such a box on the ear that *he* knocked *him* down, and had like, to have beat *his* teeth down *his* throat." We have to reflect a little to be sure to which of the persons all the *he's* and *him's* refer.

In a case of this kind we may sometimes use consistently the nominative of the pronoun to refer to one of the persons throughout the sentence, and the objective form to refer to the other; but in the sentence above we note that the first he in italic refers to *Aladdin*, and the second, the subject of the next clause, refers to *magician*; and the confusion grows to the end.

2. Gender

Of course all nouns denoting male sex will be referred to by *he* and *him* (in the singular), those denoting female sex will be referred to by *she* and *her* (in the singular), and those denoting no sex at all, by it or similar sexless pronoun.*

If the pronoun refers to "man or woman," the masculine form must be used, as in "Each of the assembled throng expressed *his* opinion" (unless the "throng" happened to be composed entirely of women).

In referring to children we usually use the neuter form, and refer to them by the use of *it* and *which.*

3. Office of Relative Pronouns

The relative pronoun performs the office of conjunction connecting a subordinate sentence to the principal sentence, as well as that of pronoun in taking the place of a noun. The relative may even take the place of a

---

* Most grammarians deduce from these sex pronouns that the English language has "gender." This is not the fact, however. Nouns in English have no gender except as they refer specifically to males or females, or to objects personified by a figure of speech.

pronoun of the first or second person. In that case the verb following the relative must correspond in person to the pronoun of which the relative is taking the place. Thus we would say, "I, who love you, can best judge you," not "I, who loves you," etc.; and "Thou, that lovest me," etc.

4. *Who, Which, That, What*

The pronoun *who* always refers to persons, *which* to things. We say nowadays, "Our Father who art in heaven, hallowed be thy name," though in former times *which* was allowable and we find it in the King James version of the Bible.

Which may refer to persons in distinguishing: between two or several, as when we say, "I cannot tell *which* of the girls I love best." It is also regularly used In referring to children, as stated above. It should always be used in referring to animals. The use of *who* or *whom* where we should expect *which* indicates personification of the object referred to, or an implied comparison to a person.

Who has *whom* as its objective case, and the case must always be determined by the construction of the sentence, principal or subordinate, in which it stands. Thus we say, "I will give it to you who are so worthy of it," but "I will give it to you whom I consider worthy of it."

Whose is the possessive form for both *who* and *what*, though *whose* in the sense of *of which* is nearly obsolete.

That as a relative pronoun refers either to persons or to things.

What is equivalent to *that which*, and its antecedent is often a general idea, sometimes expressed in the portion of the sentence which follows. Thus in the sentence, "What concerns you, concerns me," we see that the subject of the second *concerns* is the *that* implied in *what*, and the antecedent is some such general notion as 'thing."

Who, which, and what may be used interrogatively, and of course they are governed by the expected answer.

5. Errors in Use of Pronouns; Adjective, Demonstrative, Intensive, Pronouns

We must be very careful in the use of pronouns referring to persons or objects described as *each, every,* etc., the singular pronoun being required in all these cases. The proper possessive to use in referring to *one* is *one's,* though *his* is used by many writers; for example we may say, "In a Western mining town one cannot expect to have everything one's own way," or "his own way."

As a pronoun "takes the place of a noun," it is very improper to use a pronoun when the noun itself is present to fulfill its own duties. The most frequent confusion arises when we use the participle in a form in some ways resembling the absolute use, as "The candidate, being elected, was dragged all around the town by the excited citizens," not "The candidate being elected, he was dragged," etc. No educated person would say, "The man, *he* knocked me down," but in more obscure cases like the one cited above, errors are frequently made.

Besides the personal pronouns, we have "adjective pronouns," or adjectives sometimes used as pronouns, like *each, some, any,* etc. *That, this, those, these* when used as pronouns are called *demonstrative* pronouns. The *intensive* pronouns *himself, herself, yourselves,* etc., may usually be construed as adjectives or words in apposition.

6. Adjectives—The Articles

Any word which limits or qualifies a noun may properly be called an adjective. *A (an)* and *the* were formerly reckoned a separate part of speech, and were called *articles.* They serve to designate nouns as taken in a general or specific sense, but their use is liable to no special confusion.

An is used before a word beginning with a vowel sound. It is also properly used before the sound of h in a syllable not accented, but *a* is required when the syllable beginning with the sound of h is accented. We would say "a history," but "an historical work." *A* is also used instead of *an* before a word beginning with u long, as "a university," "a European," etc. In England *an* is still used, though obviously not euphonious.

7. Demonstrative Adjectives

Closely akin to the are *the* demonstrative adjectives (also used as pronouns) *that, this, these, those.* Of course the singular form must be used before a singular noun, and the plural form before a plural noun. We would not say "I do not like these kind of people," but "this kind."

8. Relative Pronouns Used as Adjectives

The relative pronouns *which* and *what* are also used as adjectives, as in "I do not know *which* boy to send," or "It is hard to tell *what* good can come of it."

9. Comparison of Adjectives

Most adjectives may express *degree* by what is called "comparison," as in referring to that which is "beautiful, more beautiful, and most beautiful." The adverbs *more* and *most* indicate these degrees of comparison, but also the endings *er* and *est* may be used and really form the regular way of indicating comparison, as in "great, greater, greatest."

Almost the only difficulty that arises in connection with the comparison of adjectives is in choosing between the endings *er* and *est* and the adverbs *more* and *most.* The determination is commonly made purely on the ground of euphony. If the endings are easily and naturally pronounced, we use them; if they are not easily and euphoniously pronounced, the two adverbs are used. We would ordinarily say "shy, shyer, shyest," but not "splendid, splendider, splendidest." There are a few irregular methods of comparison, as "good, better, best," and "bad, worse, worst."

10. Adverbs

Adverbs may regularly be formed from adjectives by adding *ly;* but there are many irregular adverbs, such as *very, much, well,* etc., which are in some cases identical with adjective forms (as *much* and *well*).

The first office of adverbs is to modify verbs, and as the notions of *time, place,* and *manner* can be connected as a usual thing only with the notions of action or condition of being, that is, with verbs, usually all words indicating time, place, or manner are adverbs or adverbial phrases. Thus we can hardly imagine a way in which such words as *here, now, how,* etc., can be applied to nouns. Some of these words, however, may be applied to adjectives, and also to other adverbs. So we speak of a word or phrase that modifies a verb, adjective, or other adverb as *adverbial.*

We have seen that a verb may be followed by an adjective in the predicate, to express a quality or limitation which is affirmed of the subject. Such an adjective really modifies the subject through the verb, and is in no sense adverbial.

11. Difficulty in Use of Adverbs

Almost the only difficulty in the use of adverbs comes from confusing predicate adjectives with adverbs. Often we see an adverb where a predicate adjective is really required.

After the verb *to be* and its parts the adjective seems so natural that no confusion is likely; but after some other verbs whose significance is varying or uncertain we often find an adverb where an adjective is required. We say "She looks beautiful," not "beautifully," since "beautiful" is a quality of the subject, not a word used in any way to describe the manner of looking. In the same way we would say "He felt bad," since there is no question of his doing or enduring the feeling badly or the reverse. *Bad* describes his condition, and hence must be an adjective. So after most verbs referring to sensations an adjective is properly used, as "It looked hot," "It sounded sweet," "It tasted sour," etc.

Though many adverbs end in ly, not all words ending in ly are adverbs, as for instance *likely*.

Adverbs may be compared sometimes as adjectives are, and often the comparative form of the adjective is used as the comparative form of the adverb without change, as "He behaved *worse* than ever before." Confusion is often obviated by using the adverbs *more* and *most* before the regular adverbial form, as "He sang more sweetly, most sweetly." The comparative endings cannot be attached to adverbs in ly, but we have *soon, sooner, soonest,* and *often, oftener, oftenest.*

12. Prepositions

Prepositions serve to introduce nouns to other nouns or to verbs, adjectives. or adverbs. They are connecting links with some meaning of their own, but depending largely for their significance upon the words they connect. A preposition and its noun, forming a prepositional phrase, are to be construed like an adjective or an adverb, and may modify any word that an adjective or adverb may modify. There are only a few of them, but those few are used in an infinite number of ways, or rather with an infinite variation of values. These variations can be mastered only by long and thoughtful reading of standard literature, with a habit of observing the uses of prepositions. Culture in the use of language finds one of its highest tests in the correct employment of prepositions.

Words commonly used as prepositions are often turned into adverbs, and sometimes into conjunctions. Whenever a word used as a preposition is found to have no part in introducing a noun, but is used for its meaning independently, it is usually an adverb. In all such phrases as "breaking *in*" "He was sent *for,*" "Come *over* to my house," the words italicized are properly parts of the verb, but since they are separated from the verb we may classify them as adverbs. Sometimes the preposition goes to the end of the sentence though it governs a relative at the beginning, as in "He was the man (whom) they sent for." Here *for* may be said to govern *whom* understood; but in the passive form of the same expression, "He was the man sent *for,*" the same word *for* appears as an adverb, or rather as a part of the verb *sent.* As the cases are analogous, we might logically say that in the sentence given above *whom* was the direct object of the verb *sent for* regarded as a single verbal expression.

Sometimes the preposition, becoming an adverb, finally appears as a conjunction introducing sentences to each other, as in "*Before* he came, she nearly starved to death." Here *before* is a conjunction; but it was previously adverb and preposition.

13. Conjunctions

All words which connect or introduce sentences have conjunctive value. Some of these words also serve as pronouns, and we call them "relative pronouns," and some serve as adverbs, and we call them "relative adverbs." Such are *who, which, what, that;* and *where, when, while, before,* etc. Another class of words serves only to express relationship between a sub-ordinate verb and its principal verb. Such are *if, unless, whether, why, that,* etc.

We also have a class of words which serves merely to associate two words or two clauses or sentences of equal rank, such as *and, or, but.* These are conjunctions in their simplest form. This class of conjunctions shows relationship without any suggestion of dependence, and in that respect these words differ from prepositions. The relative conjunctions described above are very like prepositions, practically performing for sentences the office which prepositions perform for nouns.

14. Difference Between Conjunctions and Prepositions

The distinction between conjunctions and prepositions—that prepositions introduce dependent nouns, and conjunctions introduce dependent sentences—becomes very important in the case of two conjunctions of comparison somewhat adverbial in nature, namely *as* and *than*. These two words are seldom used as prepositions, and of course as conjunctions they always imply verbs after them. In many cases these verbs are not expressed, and subjects or objects stand without their verbs. This gives rise to the supposition that the conjunctions are prepositions and the nouns or pronouns should be regarded as objects of the particle (*as* or *than*).

For example, "I will do it as soon as he (will do it)" (the first *as* is an adverb modifying *soon*, which in turn modifies the verb *do* in the main sentence, and the second *as* is an adverbial conjunction introducing the implied verb *will do,* of which *he* is the subject) ; "I will not charge more than he (will charge)"; etc.

It is probably never correct to make *as* a preposition, since we have a preposition exactly corresponding in meaning, namely *like*. And *like* is never used as a conjunction, since *as* is exactly equivalent and may always be used when a conjunction is required. Many people are in the habit of saying, "I would n't do *like* he does for anything in the world." "We should always say "like him" and "as he."*

Than is very seldom used as a preposition, but there is one case in which we are justified in making it a preposition. Milton says, "*Than whom* none higher sat." Of course if *than* is a conjunction it must here be

* Sometimes the noun or pronoun after *as* or *than* is the object rather than the subject of an implied verb, and then of course it must be in the objective case. *Example*: "They loved him more than me;" "It was better expressed by George than him."

followed by the nominative case as the subject of an implied verb, and we would have "Than who." Certainly we should say "None sat higher than he," not "than him." The difference is that after "than whom" no verb can be implied, since none has been expressed from which the implication may be made. It would be an error to construct a sentence that would compel us to go back and insert the significance of the verb after we had once passed the point at which it was required. The meaning and force of *than* take effect fully upon the relative pronoun, without reaching over to any implied verb, and a word which introduces a noun or pronoun must be a preposition, and the noun or pronoun it introduces must be in the objective case.

In this peculiar case we have another proof that English grammar is the science of the logical sequence of words in sentences.

15. Interjections

As interjections are independent words, with a relation to the sentence before or after them which is rather rhetorical than grammatical, or with no relation at all, no difficulties attend their use. There is one curious fact to be noted, however, and that is that first personal pronouns associated with interjections are in the objective case, as "Ah me!" "Oh me!" while pronouns of the second person are in the nominative case, as thou, who dwellest" etc., "O ye hypocrites," and the like. We may suppose that the attitude of the speaker in using the first person in such cases is commonly such as to imply a preposition to govern the pronoun, as in "Alas for me." In the second person we have what in Latin and Greek constitutes a separate case, the vocative. It was usually nearly the same as the nominative or subjective.

We have no peculiar form in English confined to address, and hence we may class such words with nominatives used independently. They are connected, or are identical, with some word in the accompanying sentence, but they are not in apposition, for the word with which we identify them may be in the objective case, while the nouns used in address are in effect nominative. Perhaps the best way to dispose of all such words is to class them with interjections, and make no special attempt to name their real relation to a sentence. We merely note that they have no meaning except in connection with a sentence, and so they do have a relation to that sentence even if we do not give the relation a name.

Exercise VII

Write out the third and fourth paragraphs of "The King of the Golden River" in columns, ruling three blank columns after each column of words. In the first blank column indicate what part of speech each word is; in the second blank column, write the word which each word modifies or is directly governed by, the verb after its subject, the subject after its verb, etc.; in the third blank column write the noun for which each pronoun stands and indicate the case of the pronoun, after each noun indicate its case as subject of verb, object of verb, object of preposition, in apposition, used adverbially, or used independently after each preposition, note whether it introduces an adjective or an adverbial phrase; after each adjective whether it modifies a noun direct or through the predicate; after each adverb, what part of speech it modifies; after each conjunction, whether it connects words, phrases, or sentences, and if sentences whether main (or equal), or subordinate to main.

Note—If a conjunction is copulative (connects equals), and there is not room in the second blank column to write out the phrases or sentences in full, place a star, or reference numeral, and write the desired information at the end of the paper.

Treat each verb made up of several words (compound verb) as a single word; also the infinitive with to, not marking to as a preposition but writing it in the same space with the verb. Also when noun and adjective constitute a single name, treat them as one word.

9

English Idiom

1. English Idiom

The word *idiom* means that which is peculiar. The idiom of a language consists in those peculiarities of construction in sentences and phrases which distinguish it from other languages. By extension of meaning, we call any phrase an idiom when it does not seem fully to conform to the rules of grammar, though usage has established its rights and gained for it universal recognition.

Much of the beauty and force of a language lies in its idioms,—how much we may easily perceive when we open a poor translation. The poor translator does not succeed in finding the idioms in the language into which he is translating which correspond to the idioms in the language he is seeking to translate, and a literal rendering of the words fails to convey the fullness of the meaning intended in the original. So persons who have been studying a foreign language often unconsciously pick up usages which are not appropriate to English, and their "English style" is spoiled for the time being.

There are many peculiarities which may be considered under the heading of "idiom," however, which may be common to several languages, or even to all that we know. In this chapter we wish to consider some of these peculiar uses of words in English.

Peculiar Uses of Nouns

2. Indirect Object

Sometimes after an active verb (or one which is capable of taking a direct object) we find two objects which are certainly in no way dependent upon, or equivalent to, each other. Thus if we say, "Give me the book," "book" is the direct object, but "me" appears to be an object, too. The relation is clear if we supply the preposition to and say, "Give (to) me the book." The omission of the preposition constitutes an idiom of the English language. In Latin this "indirect" object, as it is called, is distinguished by a separate case called the dative, with an ending peculiar to itself signifying *to* or *for.*

3. Adverbial Nouns

Many nouns signifying time, place, etc., are used in an adverbial sense without prepositions. To all intents and purposes they are adverbs; yet they retain the powers of nouns. Examples: "I am going *home*;" "He arrived a *day* late," or "a *day* later;" I walked a *mile* today;" "He offered Caesar the crown three *times*." The construction may usually be seen if we insert a preposition and other words and say, for example, "I am going (to my) home;" "He arrived late (by) a day;" "I walked (for, or over) a mile today;" "He offered Caesar the crown (to the number of) three times." It is not quite clear in this last sentence that our added words help the case at all. At any rate, no prepositions are implied. We must simply say that the nouns are used adverbially. The Latin has a special case for such constructions called the ablative.

4. Words Ending in *S* Sigular

By a singular idiom several nouns originally made plural by adding an s have now become singular, though the s is still retained. Among these are "news," "means," "pains," politics," "mathematics" "physics," etc., all of which must be followed by the singular verb (*is, has,* etc.).

5. Placing the Sign of the Possessive

We have already seen that it is awkward to repeat the sign of the possessive, and that modifiers of a possessive cause awkwardness. The usual way to obviate this is to regard the noun and all its modifiers as a compound word, though no hyphens be used, and place the sign of the possessive near the end of the entire expression. Thus we say, "The King of Great Britain's possession;" "For David my servant's sake;" "Give me John the Baptist's head;" etc.

6. Possessive Equivalent to Noun with *of*

The noun preceded by *of* is usually equivalent to the possessive, and in case of awkwardness we usually change the form. Thus when two possessives follow each other, we change one of them, and in place of "my friend's wife's sister," we say, "the sister of my friend's wife;" for "Chamberlain of Birmingham's seat," say "the seat of Chamberlain of Birmingham."

7. Use of Possessive with Two Nouns

When two nouns are coupled, we may put the sign of the possessive after the last one only, to show that what is possessed belongs to them in common, as in "John and Eliza's fortune." If there were two fortunes, one belonging to John and the other to Eliza, we should indicate it by saying, "John's and Eliza's fortunes."

8. Preposition Phrase or Subordinate Sentence Takes Place of Noun

A prepositional phrase, a subordinate sentence, or a participial phrase may take the place of a noun in almost any of its relations, especially as subject or object of a verb, and may have adjective modifiers in the same way that a noun has. Thus, "*For him to use the society's money* was dishonest" affords us a case in which an infinitive (*to use*) serving as a noun, the object of the preposition *for*, as a verb takes a subject in *him* and an object in *money*; and the whole unites to form the subject of the verb *was*, and is qualified by the adjective *dishonest*. The same sentence may be reconstructed a little so as to show a subordinate sentence fulfilling the same offices as the prepositional phrase, thus: "That he should use the society's money was abominable," It is a little difficult to say to what the preposition *for* and the conjunction *that* connect the words dependent upon them. To imagine an implied noun with a proper construction is not easy. We must be content with saying that these are "idioms." The following diagram pictures a sort of theory, however, in regard to one of the sentences:

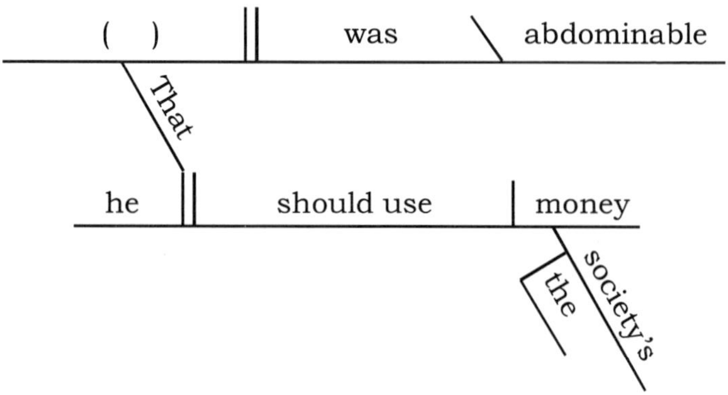

9. Adjectives Used as Nouns

Almost any adjective may be turned into a noun by placing the article *the* before it, as *the good, the great, the splendid.* We have seen that the present participle in ing is often used as a noun, though it retains powers of a verb. In the idiom of the English language there seem to be gradations of proportion between the verb quality and the noun quality. We may place *the* before the participle, and that seems to rob it of some of its verb powers. Thus we may say, "By *killing* his victim he lost all sympathy," or "By *the killing of* his victim he deprived himself of all sympathy." If we place *the* before the participle, we must follow it with a preposition to govern what was before a direct object.

10. Possessive Case with Participle

It seems to be an idiom of the English language that a participle following a preposition should be regarded as a noun rather than as an adjective, even when a noun or pronoun intervenes which might serve as the object of the preposition and take the participle as an adjective modifier. We cannot say, "I would not object to *him* doing it," but "I would not object to *his* doing it." The same is true when the participle may be the object or complement of a verb. We would say, "I do not like *his* doing it;" "It was *his* coming up that turned the tide of battle;" "Much will depend on the *pupils composing,* but more on his reading frequently." A little reflection will show that the logical object of the preposition or verb is to be found in the participle, not in the noun or pronoun.

11. Possessive Restricted to Persons

It may be noted in passing that modern usage is restricting the possessive case as far as possible to persons, or at any rate to animals, or inanimate objects which have been personified. We may say "John's bag, "Alexander's empire," "the pupil's work." We would not say "the pig-pen's side," "the rock's opening," but "the side of the pigpen," "the opening of (*or* in) the rock," etc. If we say "Chicago's beauty" we seem to personify the city; and perhaps something of the sort may be discerned in "the city's progress." "The day's work," "an hour's ride," are old forms that have survived so far.

12. Noun in Apposition with General Idea

A noun may be in apposition with a general idea contained in a variety of phrases and clauses, as when we sum up a long statement by saying, "a *state* of things which we must admit to be wholly bad;" or "a *fact* no one will deny; or "a *thing* which is obvious."

13. Two Nouns Followed by Singular Verb

Though all grammarians insist that plural subject must take the plural form of the verb, some permit two nouns joined by *and* which are so nearly alike that one may be said to be explanatory of the other, to be reckoned a singular subject, as in "Tranquility and peace dwells there." Others insist that even if the difference in such a case is slight, the conjunction *and* shows the existence of two distinct ideas, and hence the verb should be plural in form. The present writer is inclined to agree with the latter view. Yet when two nouns joined by *and* really do represent a single idea, the verb must be singular.

14. Effect on Object of Changing Active Verb to Passive

When we change such a sentence as "He offered them a pardon" into the passive form and say "They were offered a pardon," the noun "pardon" is left without a relationship to the verb which can be classed under any of the rules of grammar. In the first sentence it was the direct object of a verb; but a passive verb can have no direct object, and no preposition seems to be implied. Some grammarians condemn it as incorrect. If it is to be used, it should no doubt be classed as an idiom, and so left without explanation.

15. Nouns as Adjectives Compounded

Sometimes one noun is made to modify another as an adjective. In such cases there is a strong tendency to run the two words into one, as *coalbin, policeman, rosebush,* etc. Nouns followed by a present participle used as noun should be connected with the participle by a hyphen, as *story-writing, paper-making,* etc. But in *short story writing* no hyphen can be used, because *short* modifies *story*, not *story-writing.*

Peculiarities of Pronouns

16. Impersonal Verbs—Pronoun has no Antecedent

Though it is an established rule that every pronoun must have its antecedent (expressed or implied), there is one case in which it would be very hard to find anything that could be regarded as antecedent. When we say “It rains,” “It freezes,” “It looks like snow,” evidently *it* is as nearly devoid of meaning as a pronoun can be. It is merely a dummy subject thrown in to fill up the gap so that we may use the verb. The same is perhaps even more true when we say, “It is I,” “It is he,” “It is they,” etc., for here a neuter pronoun is made to be equivalent to a personal pronoun, and a singular pronoun to a plural. (The adverb *there* is used to fill a grammatical gap in much the same way when we say, “There is to be music tonight,” etc.)

17. Double Possessives

When we say "Here is a book of John's," we seem to have a double possessive in "of John's," but if we understand that *books* is implied—"a book of John's (books)"—the construction is clear. But when pronouns are used in a similar way, some of them slightly change their forms, and we say, "This book is hers," "Here is a book of mine," "That is ours," etc. These pronouns are not essentially different, however, from the simpler forms "my," "her," "our," etc. The changed form) enables us to avoid giving the idea that a noun; is to follow. It is a universal law of language that, so far as possible, the mind should be relieved of doubt as we pass from word to word.

18. Antecedent may follow Pronoun

Though the "antecedent" of a pronoun' may follow the pronoun instead of preceding it, the construction should always be avoided when that is possible. When the antecedent follows the pronoun, the reader or listener is kept in suspense till the explanation of the pronoun is forthcoming. This is sometimes a justifiable rhetorical artifice, as in this sentence: "There was therefore, *which* is all that we assert, a course of life pursued by them, different from that which they before led;" also in "I, John, saw all these things."

Peculiarities of Verbs

19. What is Subject of "as follows," etc.?

Every verb must have its subject, but it is not easy to find the subject of the verb in such idiomatic expressions as "as follows," "as appears," "may be," etc. Some maintain that as is a pronoun and the subject of the verb that follows, some that the subject varies and is implied from what goes before, so that we should sometimes have "as follow," for example, a plural verb; but other grammarians maintain that the impersonal pronoun "it" is implied, so that we really have "as (it) follows," etc.

20. Historical Present

In the narration of past events we sometimes use the present tense for the sake of vividness, as in this sentence: "He enters the territory of the peaceable inhabitants: he fights and conquers, takes an immense booty, which he divides among his soldiers, and returns home to enjoy a vain and useless triumph." This is called the "historical present," but it is only a figure of speech to create the illusion of events actually taking place as the narrative proceeds.

21. What is Subject of Copulative Verb?

When a copulative verb like *to be* or any of its forms comes between two nouns (or pronouns), one of which is singular and the other plural, the first is naturally the subject and the one which follows the verb is the predicate complement. But an inversion of the natural order is always allowable, so the writer may exercise his good judgment in making the verb singular or plural. Examples: "His meat was locusts and wild honey;" "A cause of the low state of industry were the restraints put upon it;" "The wages of sin is death;" "To fear no eye, and to suspect no tongue, is the great prerogative of innocence." It is natural to make the verb agree with the noun which stands nearest to it.

22. *Is with* a Conjunction?

When a single noun, followed by other nouns introduced by *with*, constitutes the subject, or when a combination of words like that which forms the subject of the preceding part of this sentence itself, stands in relation to the verb as subject, the verb should be singular according to strict grammatical rule, but as the idea is manifestly plural many of the best writers use a plural verb, and possibly they are right. In such cases we may suppose that *with* is almost a conjunction like *and*, but with a slightly different meaning. Examples: "Prosperity, with humility, renders its possessor truly amiable;" "He cannot be justified; for it is true that the prince as well as the people was (or were) blameworthy;" "The king, with the lords and commons, forms (or form) an excellent frame of government." In a sentence like the last it is evident that logically the "frame of government" was not in the "king" alone, and hence the great author who composed the sentence justly used the plural form. The case is an illustration of the conflict between formal rules of grammar and logical principles. "A number of men" used as a plural subject is an analogous example. In such cases logic usually prevails.

23. Verb After Subjects Connected by *or* Agrees with Last

When two nouns or pronouns connected by a disjunctive pronoun (*or*) form the subject of a verb, the English idiom requires agreement of the verb with the second or last, as in "He or I am the man;" "He or we are going to have that money." Such constructions are manifestly awkward, however, and should be avoided as much as possible.

24. Perfect Tense Formed with *to be*

By an old English idiom the verb *to be* is sometimes used instead of *to have* to form the perfect tenses, as in "I am come," "I was fallen," "He was cone before I got there," etc. In the last sentence *was* is better than *had*.

25. "So to Speak", Independent Infinitive

In such sentences as those containing "so to speak," the Infinitive in English seems to he used independently, very much as the participle is with the nominative absolute. The use is idiomatic, and it is hardly worth while to try to explain exactly the relationship to the rest of the sentence.

26. Predicate Adjective after Verbs of Motion

By an English idiom' verbs of motion sometimes take a predicate adjective after them, as if they were equivalent *to be*. Examples: "I shall go *mad* if this continues;" "Scipio's ghost walks *unavenged* amongst us;" "I do not enjoy going *hungry*."

Peculiar Uses of AS

27. Peculiar Uses of *as*

There is no word in the English language, perhaps, so peculiarly idiomatic in its use as *as*. We commonly regard it as an adverb or conjunction. In such phrases as "as soon as" etc., the first *as* is a simple adverb modifying *soon*, itself an adverb, and the second *as* is an adverb serving as a conjunction, as in the sentence "As soon as I see him, I will deliver your invitation." We may suppose that *soon* modifies *deliver*, the first *as* modifies *soon*, and the second *as* modifies the first *as* and also serves as a conjunction to introduce the subordinate sentence.

Some have maintained, however, that *as* is always a relative pronoun. With the pronoun *such* it is obviously a sort of relative pronoun, as in the sentence, "Such as presume to advise others, should look well to their own conduct." But there are certainly many cases in which no amount of ingenuity could explain the word as a pronoun.

One of the peculiarly idiomatic uses of as is in introducing nouns as objective or subjective predicate complements after verbs which otherwise could not easily take such complements. *Examples:* "He went out as mate and came back captain." *Mate* and *captain* are evidently the same as *he,* and therefore predicate nominatives. *As* is a sort of conjunction, but its character is purely idiomatic and not easily explained. "They regard him as their savior." In this sentence *him* is the direct object of *regard*, and *savior* is an objective complement introduced or connected to the direct object by *as*.

In such phrases as "as to those persons," we have a semi-independent phrase introduced by *as* coupled with a preposition.

In such sentences as "It would seem as if he ought to do it", as forms a compound conjunction with *if*, but implies a subordinate sentence not expressed. The full form might be, "It would seem as (it would seem) if he ought to do it," but evidently this is nonsense. Purists tell us that *as though* is not correct, since if we fill out the implied clause we have something different from what we wish to express, as *for example*—"It seems as (it would seem) though he ought to do it." Evidently *though* does not have its ordinary meaning, and accordingly we are told that *as though* is an "abominable and useless substitution for *as if,* which is natural and easily explainable." The illustration given above will show that *as if* makes as much nonsense *as though.* Usage authorizes both, and both must be considered idioms—or "compound conjunctions."

Other Peculiarities

28. An Adverb May Modify a Preposition

Our definitions do not tell us that an adverb may modify a preposition, nor that an infinitive may modify an adverb, but we can find apparent instances of both in the idioms of the language. Examples: "It lay *just below* the surface." *Just* is here an adverb modifying the preposition *below*, but it may be explained on the ground that *below* partakes also of the nature of an adverb, and in that capacity it may take an adverbial modifier. "He arrived too late to see his sister:" *To see* evidently modifies the adverb *too*— as a little reflection will show, unless we look on the infinitive as modifying the verb as it in turn is modified by the adverb *late* and that in turn by *too*. In any case, the construction is idiomatic.

29. A Word May Modify a Whole Phrase

A word may modify a whole phrase as if it were a single word, as in this sentence: "Genius can breathe *only* in the atmosphere of freedom," in which *only* modifies the entire phrase *in atmosphere* as if it were a simple adverb.

30. *When* as a Noun

An adverb may become a noun, as *when* in the sentence "Since when have you learned to hate money?" *Since* is a preposition governing *when*, which still retains its conjunctive quailties, and even something of its adverbial significance.

31. *But* as a Conjunction

A conjunction may become a preposition, as *but* does in the sentence "I will have nobody *but* him," and there are cases in which it even appears to be a relative pronoun, as in "There is not one of them but is a beauty."

32. An Adverb Following a Preposition

An adverb may follow a preposition, in such idiomatic phrases as *at once, before now,* etc., just as if it were a noun.

33. *Off* as an Adjective

Sometimes an adverb like *off* becomes an adjective, apparently, as in the idiomatic phrase "He is well off."

34. Compound Prepositions

We seem to have the force of a single preposition expressed by two words, as "*Out of* the depths," "The song rose *up to* heaven," "He jumped *on to* the table." The first of the pair in each case may be parsed as an adverb, however.

35. *Where* Equivalent to *in which*

The relative adverb *where* may be used for *in which*, as in "This is a case *where* a doctor should be called;" and other words are also often implied in its use in addition to *in which*.

36. *The* as Adverb

In such cases as "the more, the merrier," *the* appears to be an adverb. The use is purely idiomatic. In Anglo-Saxon it was a different word from the article.

37. Two Negatives Make an Affirmative

In some languages two negatives serve to Intensify the negation, but the English language follows strict logical principles in this matter, and so in English two negatives destroy each other, or create an affirmative. *Examples:* "His language, though inelegant, is not ungrammatical,"—that is, it is "grammatical;" "I never did repent of doing good, *nor* shall *not* now" an evident absurdity; "Tasso, *no* more than Raphael, was *not* born in a republic"—another absurdity. Poetic license at times justifies the double negative, but it is not to be justified in prose unless the meaning is intended to be taken as literally expressed. The first example given above is, of course, a good sentence, since we often wish to look at a thought from the negative as well as from the positive side.

38. Use of *shall* and *will* (*should* and *would*)

Use of Shall and Will (should and would). As has already been said, simple prediction of the future is indicated by the use of *shall* with the first person, and *will* with the second and third persons. If we wish to express willingness in any degree whatever, we may use *will* with the first person, as, "If you wish, I will go to town tomorrow;" or in any sentence in which the words "am willing to" could be substituted with any propriety.

Shall is used with the second and third persons to indicate compulsion, as "You shall do it, whether you wish to or not." Any case which assumes that the person speaking will use his will power to induce or compel calls for *shall* in place of *will.*

Shall may also be used (and indeed is almost required) in asking a question for which the anticipated answer is *I shall* or *shall not,* or *we shall.* Thus we say, "Shall you go to the opera tonight?" Answer, "I shall," The same principle applies to indirect discourse, as "He says he shall go."

Shall is seldom, if ever, wrongly used, but many good writers and most conversationalists use *will* more or less with the first person for mere prediction when there is no emphasis on the word and especially when the use of *shall* might seem to imply emphasis of some kind. Purists condemn this usage. The fact is, instinct does not warn us of any special difference between those cases in which willingness may be appropriately expressed, and those in which the nature of the ideas seems to exclude willingness. Nearly all critics condemn the practice, and nearly all English speaking people (except, perhaps, those of England, not including Scotland and Ireland) are addicted to it.

All that has been said of the use of *shall* and *will* applies with equal force to the past tenses, *should* and *would.* We may add that "should" frequently signifies "ought," as in "You should say 'It is I.' " To avoid giving this significance we often use *would* after a first personal pronoun for mere prediction, as in "We would (naturally) say "It is I'."

39. Such Words as *perfect, circular, complete,* not Compared

The comparative and superlative degrees are not appropriate to such adjectives as *perfect, circular, complete,* etc., since they express an absolute, not a relative quality. What is *perfect* is *absolutely perfect,* and cannot be *more perfect.* Something may be *more nearly perfect,* however, *more nearly complete, more nearly circular.* By a sort of syncope, the *nearly* is often omitted, and while *more circular* can perhaps never be found in good writers, and *more perfect* seldom, *more complete* is very commonly used. The general principle applies to many other adjectives and some adverbs.

40. How Use or Omission of *a* Causes Difference in Meaning

The difference in meaning that may result from the use

or omission of the small word a is illustrated in the following: "He behaved with little reverence," and "He behaved with a little reverence."

41. Idiomatic Use of *and*

And has a peculiar idiomatic use in parenthetical sentences such as the following: "The sky is changed (*and* such a change!)"

42. Idiomatic Phrases

In the following phrases words have meanings which they do not have in other connections: "by and by," "at all events," "ever and anon," "here and there," "at large," "to be sure," "by the way," or "by the bye," "upon the whole," "at length," "of course," "all along," "all in all," "to bear in mind," "to make bold," "to come to one's-self," "to come to hand," "in point of fact," "to carry out," "to come about," "to come by," "to take after," "for instance," "as a matter of course."

In conclusion let us remark that idioms in no way interfere or conflict with the logical relationships of words, but merely illustrate the peculiar values and offices which words may have, or the unusual meanings attached to them in certain connections. In many cases these idioms are the direct result of the instinctive self-assertion of logical principles in cases in which the mechanical reasoner or follower of rules is misled by a false analogy. "Analogy" plays an important part in language; but when it conflicts with "logical principle" it must inevitably yield. To real logical principles there are and can be no exceptions whatever: when we find exceptions, we should realize that we have not discovered the real logical principle, or our method of stating it is faulty.

10

Conclusion

A sentence is like an arch. It must rest upon two solid foundations, the subject noun and the predicate verb. To be a good arch, every word must fit nicely into its particular niche. One word which does not fit perfectly may cause the whole arch to fall. We may even have arch upon arch in an architecture complicated and beautiful, but each word, like each brick, must be of faultless material, and moreover must be so precisely adapted in form as to fill the space allotted to it without being anything but just what is required of it.

In such a comparison as this we find our two universal laws, the necessity for two bases—the subject and the predicate, and the requirement that every word be adjusted to a perfect relation with every other word without a break or flaw of any kind. These two requirements cover the entire subject.

In making a sentence we must take account of two things, the individual meanings of the words and the relationship which they are to hear to each other. The meanings are given us by usage. We must acquire them as we acquire bricks. But once possessed of an ample supply, we must exercise our mental ability in fitting them together, selecting just the right one for each little niche and turn. If we have the mind to understand, each problem may be solved as we go along. We may look at our niche and then hunt about till we find the right word to fill it. We may try one, and if that does not serve, we may try another. Unless we are pretty nearly right, our arch will not stand at all; and if it is poorly put together and awkward, no doubt we shall realize it as we look it over, as well as any one would.

Our study of grammar should be practical. First, our teacher should go over the entire arch, saying, "For this point select this kind of a word; make this fit here nicely; this corner will go into this depression easily." He has had experience, and we try to benefit by his experience. But that is not enough. We must build for ourselves, and when we have difficulty we must ask for help. When we shall have served our apprenticeship, we shall become master masons. No amount of study of theory will make us good workmen without practice; and we should have a teacher to suggest and explain when we get into trouble.

In studying grammar it is first necessary that we understand the general principles on which sentences are constructed; and then we should train our minds to logical analysis of word relationships. It is utterly impossible to foresee every difficulty and provide for it. We must have a mind capable of original solutions. We may be put on our guard against errors that seem natural to all human kind, errors which no doubt we shall commit ourselves; but we should never correct an error *because we are told that we ought,* but because we see that not to correct it will be fatal to our purpose to express our ideas. We may forget what we have been told; we may even lose faith in our authority; but if we can solve the problem for ourselves, as we solve the problem of the multiplication of 15 by 4, we always have it in our power to find out for ourselves even if we do forget what we have been told or otherwise have learned; and what we have logically demonstrated we will not doubt.

The author of this book, therefore, strongly recommends the study of grammar by original processes, not by authorities and rules. All that a rule can do is to aid the memory in regard to a certain peculiarity; and when the peculiarity is perfectly familiar, we do not need the rule or the definition, and may safely forget both. Not until we have reached the point at which we can go on just as well without remembering a single rule or definition, can we be said to have become "accomplished" writers.

TEST EXERCISE IN GRAMMAR

Ruskin's "The King of the Golden River" has been selected for illustrative analysis because it is simple, and because Ruskin was not only a correct but an accomplished architect of sentences. His work is really beautiful in its nice adjustment, yet it is perfectly natural and unconscious.

The notes and questions are intended as a practical illustration of the principles that have been set forth in the preceding pages, and also as an exercise upon them. The first time a peculiar construction is met, it is commented upon; after that for the most part the student is directed by questions. The numbers in parentheses refer to sections in the preceding discussion of grammar, while the question numbers refer to words in the text above indicated by superior figures. "Construe" means, Tell what part of speech a word is and give its construction.

RUSKIN'S THE KING OF THE GOLDEN RIVER

1. In a secluded and mountainous part of Stiria there[1] was[2], in old time, a valley of the most surprising and luxuriant fertility. It was surrounded, on all sides, by steep and rocky mountains, rising into peaks which were always covered with snow, and[3] from[4] which a number of torrents descended in constant cataracts. One[5] of these fell westward[6], over the face of a crag so high[7] that[8], when the sun had set to everything else[9] and all below[10] was darkness, his beams still shone full[11] upon this waterfall, so that it looked like[12] a shower of gold. It

was, therefore[13], called, by the people of the neighborhood, the Golden River[14]. It was strange[15] that none of these streams fell into the valley itself[16]. They all[17] descended on the other side of the mountains, and wound away through broad plains and by populous cities. But[18] the clouds were drawn so constantly to the snowy hills, and rested so softly in the circular hollow, that[19] in time of drought and heat, when[20] all the country round was burnt up, there was[21] still rain in the little valley; and its crops were so heavy, and its hay so high, and its apples so red, and its grapes so blue and its wine so rich, and its honey so sweet, that[22] it was a marvel to every one who beheld it, and was[23] commonly called the Treasure[24] Valley.

2. The whole of this little valley belonged to three brothers, called Schwartz[25], Hans, and Gluck. Schwart and Hans, the two elder brothers, were[26] very ugly men[27], with[28] overhanging eyebrows and small dull eyes, which were always half shut[29], so[30] that you couldn't see into *them*, and always fancied[31] they saw very far into *you*. They lived by farming the Treasure Valley, and very good farmers[32] they were. They killed everything that[33] did not pay for its eating. They shot the blackbirds, because[34] they pecked the fruit; and killed the hedgehogs, lest they should suck the cows; they poisoned the crickets for eating the crumbs in the kitchen; and smothered the cicadas, which used to sing all summer[35] in the lime trees. They worked their servants[36] without any wages, till[37] they would not work any[38] more, and then quarreled with them, and turned them out[39] of doors without paying them. It would have been very odd[40], if with such a farm, and such a system of farming, they hadn't got very rich; and very rich[41] they *did* get. They generally contrived to keep their corn by them till[42] it was very dear, and then

sell[43] it for twice[44] its value; they had heaps of gold lying[45] about on their floors, yet it was never known that they had given so much as[46] a penny[47] or a crust in[48] charity; they never went to mass; grumbled[49] perpetually at paying tithes, and were, in a word[50], of so cruel[51] and grinding a temper, as[52] to receive from all those with whom they had any dealings, the nickname of[53] the "Black Brothers."

3. The youngest brother, Gluck[54], was as completely opposed, in both appearance and character, to his seniors as could[55] possibly[56] be imagined or desired. He was not above twelve years[57] old, fair, blue-eyed, and kind[58] in temper tor[59] every living thing. He did not, of course[60], agree particularly well[61] with his brothers, or rather[62] they did not agree with *him*. He was usually appointed to the honorable office of[63] turnspit, when there was[64] anything to roast, which[65] was not often[66]; for[67], to do[68] the brothers[69] justice, they were hardly less sparing[70] upon themselves than[71] upon other people. At other times he used to clean the shoes, floors, and sometimes[72] the plates, occasionally getting what[73] was left on them, by[74] way of encouragement, and a wholesome quantity of dry blows, by way of education.

4. Things went on[75] in this manner for a long time. At last came[76] a very wet summer, and everything went wrong[77] in the country around.[78] The hay had hardly been got in, when[79] the hay-stacks were floated[80] bodily[81] down[82] to the sea by an inundation; the vines were cut to pieces with the hail; the corn was all[83] killed by a black blight; only[84] in the Treasure Valley, as usual, all was safe. As it had rain when there was rain nowhere else, so it had sun when there was sun nowhere else.[85] Everybody came to buy corn at the farm, and went away

pouring[86] maledictions on the Black Brothers. They asked what they liked, and got it, except[87] from the poor people, who could only beg, and several[88] of whom were starved[89] at their very door, without the slightest regard or notice.

5. It[90] was drawing toward winter, and very cold weather,[91] when one day the two elder brothers had gone out, with their usual warning to little Gluck, who was left to mind the roast, that[92] he was to let nobody in,[93] and give[94] nothing out. Gluck sat down quite[95] close[96] to the fire, for it was raining very hard, and the kitchen walls were by no means dry or comfortable[97] looking. He turned and turned, and the roast got nice[98] and brown. "What a pity[99]," thought Gluck, "my brothers never ask anybody to dinner! I'm sure, when they've got such[100] a nice piece of mutton as this[101], and nobody else has got so much as a piece[102] of dry bread, it would do their hearts good[103] to have somebody to eat it with them."

6. Just as[104] he spoke, there came[105] a double knock at the house[106] door, yet heavy[107] and dull, as though[108] the knocker had been tied up—more like a puff than a knock.

7. "It must be the wind," said[109] Gluck; "nobody else would venture to knock double knocks at our door."

8. No[110]; it wasn't the wind; there[111] it came again very hard[112] and what[113] was particularly astounding, the knocker seemed to be in a hurry, and not[114] to be in the least afraid[115] of the consequences. Gluck went to the window, opened it, and put his head out to see who[116] it was.

9. It was the most extraordinary[117] looking little gentleman he[118] had ever seen in his life. He had a very

large nose, slightly brass-coloured; his cheeks were very round, and very red, and might have warranted a supposition that[119] he had been blowing a refractory fire for the last eight-and-forty hours; his eyes twinkled merrily through long silky eyelashes, his mustaches curled twice round[120] like a corkscrew on each side of his mouth, and his hair, of a curious mixed pepper-and-salt colour, descended far over his shoulders. He was about[121] four feet six[122] in height, and wore a conical-pointed[123] cap of nearly the same altitude, decorated with a black feather some[124] three feet[125] long. His doublet was prolonged behind into something resembling a violent exaggeration of what is now termed a "swallow tail," but was much obscured by the swelling fold of an enormous black, glossy-looking cloak, which must have been very much[126] too long in[127] calm weather, as the wind, whistling round the old house, carried it clear[128] out from the wearer's shoulders to about four times his own length[129].

10. Gluck was so perfectly paralyzed by the singular appearance of his visitor, that[130] he remained fixed[131], without uttering a word, until the old gentleman, having performed another[132] and a more energetic concerto on the knocker, turned round to look after his fly-away cloak. In so doing he caught sight of Gluck's little yellow head jammed[133] in the window, with its mouth and eyes very wide[134] open indeed[135].

11. "Hello!" said the little gentleman, "that's[136] not the way to answer the door; I'm wet, let[137] me in."

12. To do[138] the little gentleman justice, he was wet. His feather hung down between his legs like a beaten puppy's tail, dripping[139] like an umbrella; and from the

ends of his mustaches the water was running into his waistcoat pockets, and out again like a mill-stream.

13. "I beg pardon, sir," said Gluck, "I'm very sorry[140], but I really can't."

14. "Can't what!" said the old gentleman.

15. "I can't let you in, sir[141],—I can't, indeed[142]; my brothers would beat me to death, sir, if I thought of such a thing. What do you want, sir?"

16. "Want?" said the old gentleman, petulantly. "I want fire, and shelter; and there's your great fire there blazing, crackling, and dancing on the walls, with nobody to feel it. Let me in, I say; I only want to warm myself."

17. Gluck had had his head, by this time, so long[143] out of the window, that he began to feel it[144] was really unpleasantly[145] cold, and when he turned, and saw the beautiful fire rustling and roaring, and throwing[146] long bright tongues up the chimney as if it were licking its chops at the savory smell of the leg of mutton, his heart melted within him that it should be burning away for nothing. "He does[147] look *very* wet," said little Gluck; "I'll just let him in for a quarter of an hour." Round he went to the door, and opened it; and as the little gentleman walked in, there came[148] a gust of wind through the house that[149] made the old chimneys totter[150].

REFERENCES

1. *There* is an "anticipative" adverb, because it serves to anticipate the subject.
2. The subject of *was is valley.*
3. *And* connects what two sentences?
4. *From* connects *which* to *descended.*

5. *One* as an adjective pronoun represents *cataract* implied in the plural *cataracts*; or it may be regarded as an adjective modifying *cataract* implied.
6. *Westward* is what part of speech?
7. *High* is an adjective modifying *crag*, though it follows its noun. What is the regular position for an adjective?
8. *That* introduces the sentence *beams . . shone* through the adverb *so* which modifies *high*.
9. What part of speech is *else*?
10. *Below* appears to be an adjective modifying the noun *all*, though in its nature it is adverbial. It is a condensed form of "all that was below," in which *below* appears as an adverb.
11. *Full* is a predicate adjective (cf. 104).
12. Is *like* a preposition or an adjective?
13. *Therefore* is an adverb modifying *called*, though it has some conjunctive value with reference to the preceding sentence.
14. *Golden*, though an adjective, should be treated as a part of the single name "Golden River."
15. What is the construction of *strange*? Note that it is qualified by a subordinate sentence introduced by *that*.
16. What part of speech is *itself*? (60).
17. What part of speech?
18. *But* connects the sentence following to the ideas in what precedes. *However* may do the same, though an adverb. The logic of ideas does not stop with the sentence, for words have relations from sentence to sentence and paragraph to paragraph as truly as within the sentence.
19. What verb does *that* introduce, and through what adverbs does it connect?

20. As an adverb, what does *when* modify?
21. What is the subject of *was*?
22. Between what words does *that* serve as a connective?
23. What is the subject of *was*?
24. What part of speech is *Treasure*?
25. What is the case of *Schwartz*? (cf. 22 and 105).
26. What is the subject of *were*?
27. What is the construction of *men*? (22).
28. To what does *with* connect its nouns.
29. What part of speech is *shut*?
30. What does so modify?
31. What is the subject of *fancied*?
32. What is the case of *farmers*?
33. What part of speech is *that*, and what is its construction? (60).
34. Between what words does *because* show relationship?
35. How is *summer* used? (81).
36. What is the construction of *servants*?
37. Construe *till*.
38. What part of speech is *any*?
39. Construe *out*. (112).
40. Construe *odd*.
41. *Rich* is a predicate adjective preceding the verb.
42. Construe *till*.
43. *Sell* is an infinitive with *to* omitted, same construction as *to keep*.
44. Notice that *twice* is an adjective here. It may be an adverb.
45. Construe *lying*.
46. Analyse *so much as*. (69 and 105).

47. What is the construction of *penny*? Supply implied words.
48. *In* connects *charity* to *given.*
49. What is the subject of *grumbled?*
50. *In a word* is idiomatic, and partially independent (cf. 103).
51. Observe the placing of descriptive adjectives before *a* in order that they may be modified by the adverb *so.*
52. Note *as* introducing an infinitive. (105).
53. Note that *of* here connects two words exactly equivalent.
54. What is the construction of *Gluch*? (20).
55. What is the subject of the verb of which *could* is a part, and what constitutes the entire verb? (cf. 97).
56. Construe *possibly.*
57. Is *years* governed by *above*? (cf. 81).
58. Notice that an adjective may be modified by a prepositional phrase.
59. Construe *to.*
60. An idiom,—used independently.
61. Construe *well.*
62. *Rather* is here used idiomatically. We may supply a verb, or connect it to *did* (not) *agree* as an adverb.
63. How is *of* used?
64. What is the subject of *was*?
65. The antecedent of *which* is a general idea, or a word like *thing* implied.
66. Do you think *often* an adverb or an adjective? (cf. 65.).
67. Construe *for.*

68. Here we have an independent infinitive, not unlike the participle with nominative absolute, (cf. 103).
69. Construe *brothers.* (80).
70. *Sparing* is here an adjective pure and simple, not a participle.
71. What is implied after *than*?
72. What does the adverb *sometimes* modify?
73. For what does the pronoun *what* stand? (58).
74. What does *by* modify?
75. Construe *on.* (66).
76. What is the subject of *came* and how do you account for its position?
77. Construe *wrong.* (104).
78. What part of speech is *around* here? As what other part of speech do we commonly find it?
79. With what adverb does *when* have a relationship?
80. What voice? Cf. question 89.
81. Is *bodily* adjective, or adverb?
82. Construe *down.*
83. Is *all* adjective, adverb, pronoun, or noun? In what different ways may *all* be used?
84. What does *only* modify? (107).
85. Construe *else* and compare with question 9.
86. Construe *pouring.*
87. *Except* may here be construed as a conjunction introducing an implied verb, or a preposition introducing a prepositional phrase (*from . . . people*) as if it were a noun.
88. What part of speech is *several*?
89. Notice the difference in meaning if we used *had starved* here in place of *were starved.* The participle becomes almost an adjective pure and simple.

90. What is the antecedent of *it*? (94).
91. *Weather* is predicate nominative after *it was* implied from *it was drawing*—an unusual and irregular construction. Quote another example of a similar construction.
92. *That* introduces a subordinate sentence in apposition to the noun *warning*, or explanatory of it.
93. *In* is evidently an adverb. Give three examples of prepositions used as adverbs.
94. *Give* is an infinitive subordinate to what implied words?
95. Purists do not approve of the use of *quite* in the sense of *very*, but only in the sense of *completely*.
96. *Close* is a predicate adjective, but almost an adverb in sense.
97. When an adjective like *comfortable* comes before a present participle we may treat the participle as a noun, but when an adjective comes before a past participle we must connect it to the participle by a hyphen—else the adverb is required, as *hard-headed*, but *badly dressed*.
98. *Nice* and *brown*—why adjectives?
99. Construe *pity*. What words are implied?
100. Notice that the adjective *such* comes before *a*.
101. What is the case of *this*? Supply implied words.
102. Construe each word in the phrase *so much as a piece*. (105).
103. *Good* is a noun here. Construe.
104. *Just* modifies *as*, which modifies what?
105. What is the advantage of the transposed form of the sentence?
106. Note that *house* is here a pure adjective. A hyphen might be used to unite it to *door*.

107. What do *heavy* and *dull* modify?
108. Account for *though.* (105).
109. Notice that the words spoken form the object of *said.*
110. No, like an interjection, is equivalent to -a condensed negative sentence.
111. What kind of an adverb is *there*?
112. Is *hard* an adjective or an adverb?
113. What idea is the antecedent of *what*? (59).
114. What does *not* modify?
115. Construe *afraid.*
116. Why not *whom*?
117. Construe *extraordinary.*
118. The conjunction *that* is implied before *he.*
119. Construe *that.*
120. What part of speech is *round*? What other part of speech is it often?
121. If *about* is an adverb, how could you account for it? (81).
122. Construe *six*, supplying implied words.
123. Compare with question 97, noticing the hyphen.
124. *Some* may be regarded as an adverb here. What other parts of speech may it be?
125. Construe *feet.* Give other examples of nouns used in a similar way.
126. *Much* modifies *too.*
127. What does *in* modify?
128. Is *clear* an adjective or an adverb?
129. Construe each word *about . . .length.*
130. To what word does *that* show relation?
131. *Fixed* must be treated as a predicate adjective.
132. What does *another* modify?

133. Construe *jammed.*
134. *Wide* seems to be between an adjective and an adverb.
135. *Indeed* is an adverb modifying *wide*, or *open* as modified by *wide*?
136. Construe each word in *that's.*
137. Is *let* an auxiliary here? What is its subject?
138. *To do* is a sort of independent infinitive (103).
139. Construe *dripping.*
140. Construe *sorry.*
141. *Sir* is a noun, independent nominative used in address.
142. Construe *indeed.*
143. *Long* is here an adverb. Why?
144. What is the antecedent of *it*, and what conjunction is implied before it?
145. Construe *unpleasantly.*
146. What does *throwing* modify?
147. What is the value of the auxiliary *does* here?
148. Is *came* in a subordinate sentence?
149. What part of speech is *that*?
150. What kind of an adjective is *totter?* (22)

PUNCTUATION

Punctuation is an important, though not indispensable, aid to grammar. It is a modern device, for the ancients had no punctuation whatever; but a mastery of it adds wonderfully to the clearness and force of language in expressing ideas effectively.

The best way in which to learn it is to form the habit of observing the punctuation of standard literature as one reads. The number of rules in common manuals of punctuation is so great as to confuse rather than to aid the mind. It is better to drill on a very few cardinal principles, and trust to instinct and observation for cases not covered by such principles.

1. Capital Letters

Every noun which is the name of a single individual is called a *proper* noun, and should begin with a capital letter, while a noun *which* designates a class of individuals is called a common noun, and begins with a small letter unless the capital be required by its position in the sentence.

Examples: John, Mary, Europe, Washington, (the) Coliseum, etc., are proper nouns; cow, west, country, sun, battle, etc., are all common nouns. If, however, a common noun by continued use designates a particular object or place, by such fuse it becomes a proper noun and must be written with a capital letter, as (the) *South* used to designate the southern part of the United States, (the) *West* used to designate the western part of the United States, (the) *Orient* used to designate Asia and adjacent territory, etc. (The) *sun* and (the) *moon* logically ought to appear with capitals, but their use is so common that the capitals are not employed.

Adjectives derived from proper names are also written

with capitals, as *European*, Western (referring to the western part of the United States), *Oriental,* etc.

There is an old rule that every sentence begins with a capital letter; but this is true only if the preceding sentence ends with a period.

Every line of poetry begins with a capital letter.

Common nouns are sometimes written with capital letters to show emphasis, or when by a figure of speech the writer wishes to give them the dignity of proper nouns, as, "The three cardinal principles of sentence-making are Unity, Mass, and Coherence;" "He was very fond of Art (spelled with a capital letter)."

Quotations and statements complete in themselves as sentences are begun with capital letters. Examples: He said, "Now is the time to make your fortune;" The great rule for business success is, Do well whatever you have to do, cost what it may.

Incomplete quotations are not begun with capitals. Example: He sent word home to have a good dinner ready; "for," said he, "I have not had anything fit to eat in three days."

2. The Period

Ordinary sentences, if complete, are ended with a period. A group of words cannot end with a period unless it contains a principle subject and a principle predicate, expressed or understood. Groups of words which omit subject or predicate are not complete sentences, and if used at all they must be treated as exclamations and be followed by exclamation points. Carlyle and some others ignore this rule.

(The old rule that every complete sentence begins

with a capital letter and ends with a period is not strictly correct, for many sentences grammatically complete in every way end with colons,' semi-colons, and even with commas, if the ideas they contain are closely connected with those in adjoining sentences. Such connected sentences cannot in most cases be reckoned compound sentences).

Every abbreviation should be followed by a period. Examples: D.D., Mr., LL. D., e. g., lb., Messrs.

Formerly the Roman numerals (I, II, III, etc.), were followed by periods, but that usage is now being discontinued.

3. The Comma

The art of punctuation lies in the skilful use of the comma more than In anything else. It shows delicate shades of meaning which cannot be expressed without it and is very important in making the logical relationship of words quite clear.

The chief use of the comma is to set off groups of words, which are known as phrases, clauses, or subordinate sentences. Each group, if separate in idea from a preceding or following group, is set off by commas.

The comma is also used to show that a modifying word or phrase passes over intervening words or phrases and modifies some word beyond them.

These two general services cover nearly the whole subject of the use of the comma. A comma should never be used unless it helps to make the meaning clear. Whenever by disconnecting a group of words from other words in a sentence, the words within the group itself can be more closely united relatively to the rest of the sentence, the writer is justified in using the comma whether he can find a rule for it or not; and if he wishes to emphasize the disconnection of the ideas expressed by different groups of words, he is justified in using a comma to separate them. Again, if one word seems to be more closely connected with the word it modifies than other words which are equally modifiers, that word may be disconnected so that all the words may appear to be equal. In short, the comma is used to show the relative connection between words, and especially between groups of words, such as prepositional and participial phrases and subordinate sentences.

We will now give a few specific rules with illustrations.

Rule 1. Several words, all of which modify equally, or stand in the same relationship to, some other word, are separated by commas.

Examples: He was a great, good, noble man. (The three adjectives *great, good*, and *noble*, all modify *man* equally. The commas would be used just the same if the last two were connected by *and*, as we may see in the preceding sentence, though some writers inconsistently omit the comma before *and*. If, however, there are only two, and they are connected by *and*, or if there are several, all connected by *and*, no comma is used; as in, "He was a great and good man," or, "He was a great and good and noble man.")

Men, women and children ran for their lives. (Here the three nouns *men, women*, and *children*, are all equally the subject of *ran*.)

Rule 2. When adjectives modify a noun unequally, one modifying the meaning of the noun as first qualified by another adjective, no comma is used to separate the two adjectives.

Example: The poor old man ran for his life. (Here *poor* modifies the meaning of *old man*, not *man* alone, and *the* modifies *man* as first modified by *poor* and *old*.)

(*The* is never set off by a comma when it is one of the several adjectives modifying a noun.)

Rule 3. Any phrases or clauses which have an equal relationship to any following word are separated not only from each other but from the word they modify by a comma or commas.

Examples: An illustration of this principle is to be found in the statement of Rule 1, (*some other*) *word* being the object equally of the verb *modify* and the preposition *to*. (A structure like this is somewhat awkward and is to be justified only in very exact scientific statements.)

Men, women, and children, all gave of what they had. (There is a comma between *children* and *all* to show that *all* refers to or summarizes the three nouns preceding it, bearing the same relation to one that it does to the others.)

(The three rules preceding are illustrations of the second of our cardinal principles. The same principle appears incidentally in examples of phrase grouping, illustrating the first great cardinal principle, which is elucidated by the following rules.)

Rule 4. A subordinate sentence, or a participial phrase, is set off from the main sentence by a comma or commas if it is merely explanatory, but if it is restrictive, no commas are required.

(***Note.*** This is the most difficult and important rule we shall give, and it should be thoroughly mastered.)

Examples: There is the man who provoked him. (The subordinate sentence "who provoked him" modifying *man* is absolutely necessary to the full meaning, that is, it restricts the meaning of *man* instead of being merely an explanatory addition. Therefore no comma is required.)

Do you remember Jenny, who was at the lake last summer? Tin this sentence the meaning would be complete if we stopped with *Jenny* and placed a period after that word. The subordinate sentence merely throws in an additional explanation, and therefore is set off by a comma.)

The man who has mastered his subject will rule in his profession (This is another case of a restrictive subordinate sentence. If it were omitted, the remaining parts of the sentence would make nonsense. The relative clause restricts the meaning of *man*—It is not any man, but "the man who has mastered his profession.")

That man yonder, who was a millionaire last year, is almost ready to commit suicide. (If the subordinate sentence were omitted, the words left would still make complete sense. The relative clause is thrown in by way of additional explanation, and therefore is set off by commas.)

I love the lake because it is so beautiful.

I love the lake, because it is so beautiful.

(The use or omission of the comma in the preceding sentence indicates a difference in meaning. If the emphasis is on the subordinate sentence "because it is so beautiful," no comma is needed; but if the emphasis is on the main sentence, "I love the lake," and the subordinate sentence is thrown in merely by may of additional explanation, a comma should be used.)

I know where you are hiding.

I am going over there, where you are hiding.

(In the first sentence the subordinate clause is a necessary part of the sentence, and so is not set off by commas, while in the second "where you are hiding" merely explains *there*.)

I know a man called John.

Do you see that tree, just hanging over the edge of the mountain?

(In the first sentence the participial phrase "called John" restricts the meaning of *man*, and is absolutely necessary to the sentence. Therefore no comma is needed. In the second sentence, the participial phrase is additional and explanatory, and the sentence would be complete without it. Therefore it is set off by a comma. If *that tree* had been *the tree* the phrase would have been restrictive, as it would have been required to indicate what tree. As it is, the word *that* implies that the tree is pointed out by the speaker, and the following clause is thrown in by way of explanation.)

Rule 5. Subordinate sentences and phrases which are transposed from their natural position in the sentence are usually set off by commas.

Examples: Where I go, there ye shall come also.

(In this sentence the natural position for "where I go" would be after the verb and *there* would then be omitted.)

After due consideration, they decided to give their notes.

(A prepositional phrase naturally follows the word it modifies, in this case the verb *decided.* As it is transposed to a place before the subject it is set off by a comma.)

Rule 6. All words and phrases thrown in by way of explanation, or used independently in a sentence, are set off by commas.

Examples: I prefer, on the whole, to have my own way. (Here the phrase "on the whole" follows the word it modifies in natural order, but as it is thrown in merely by way of explanation, it is set off by commas.)

Yes. John. I shall go tomorrow. (In this sentence *John* is used independently, as it is the name of the person addressed; hence it is set off by commas.)

Christ, the great teacher, said, "Come unto me." (The words "the great teacher" are thrown in to explain Christ. Here *teacher* is a noun in apposition with the noun *Christ.*)

Rule 7. When a noun in apposition with another noun is so closely related to that noun as really to form a single name with it, no comma should be used. The same rule applies to adjectives preceded by *the* following a name.

Examples: William the Conqueror. Richard the lion-hearted, Frederick the great.

4. The Semi-colon

When several sentences are closely connected in meaning, they are often separated by semi-colons to indicate a closer relationship than would be indicated if they were separated by periods. Compound sentences connected by *but* are separated by a semi-colon if the two parts are strongly contrasted. Phrases, or groups of words, are often separated by semi-colons when they are themselves subdivided by commas.

Examples (taken from Macaulay, a master In the use of the colon and the semi-colon)

He was a soldier; he had risen by war.

Its triumphs added nothing to his fame; its increase added nothing to his means of overawing his enemies; its great leader was not his friend.

This constitution in former days used to be the envy of the world; it was the pattern for politicians; the theme of the eloquent; the meditation of the philosopher in every part of the world.

The lines are few, the coloring faint; but the general air and expression is caught.

It burned down the city; but it burned out the plague.

It would be easy to indicate many points of resemblance between the subjects of Diocletian and the people of the Celestial Empire, where, during many centuries, nothing has been learned or unlearned; where government, where education, where the whole system of life, is a ceremony; where knowledge forgets to increase and multiply, and, like the talent buried in the earth, or the pound wrapped up in a napkin, experiences neither waste nor augmentation.

It is despised and rejected of men; and every device and invention of ingenuity or idleness is set up in opposition, or in preference to it.

As a simple example of the last clause in the rule, we offer the following: The list of hero kings of England includes Alfred, called the great; Richard the lion-hearted, who did yeoman's service in the crusades; William the Conqueror; and, if we may add a queen, Elizabeth.

5. The Colon

The nature and use of the colon are not well understood by ordinary writers, and this mark of punctuation is seldom required in ordinary writing. It would be well to dispense with it except in cases where its use is clearly comprehended.

The colon signifies that what precedes is logically equivalent to what follows. It is used in the formal introduction of "quotations, especially after such phrases as "as follows." The introduction states that *he spoke*, the quotation following gives the words of his speech. One is the equivalent of the other.

It will be seen that in most cases the colon has a special meaning of its own, and to say that it indicates a pause more abrupt than the semi-colon is usually incorrect.

Examples: The wind raged, and the rain beat against the window: it was a miserable day. (The last sentence summarizes the preceding. It will be observed that the colon closes what is really a complete sentence; and the sentence which follows is also complete.)

One thing thou lackest: go thy way, sell whatsoever thou hast, and give to the poor. (Again we see the logical equivalence of the two sentences separated by the colon.)

(***Note.*** The equality between the ideas in sentences

separated from each other by colons may be of a great variety of kinds. If the writer wishes to balance two sentences against each other and indicate that one offsets the other, that is, that one is equal to the other in its value as an idea, he may use the colon between the two. Macaulay, who constantly uses the balanced structure as a rhetorical device, employs the colon again and again to indicate that he means to balance his first sentence against his second, though in many cases one is just opposite in meaning to the other. The following are examples:)

Hatred and revenge eat into the heart: yet his aspect and language exhibit nothing but philosophical moderation.

The following generation produced indeed no second Dante: but it was eminently distinguished by general intellectual activity.

This is strange: and yet the strangest is behind.

(In very long and complicated sentences the colon may also be used to show greater separation than is indicated by semi-colons in the same sentence.)

6. The Separation of Sentences

We have seen that the colon has a more or less special use; but all sentences may be separated by periods, by semi-colons, or by commas, according to the closeness of the thought which they contain. If the thought in two sentences is clearly distinct, each sentence must begin with a capital letter and end with a period; if we wish to show that two sentences are a little more closely associated in thought than other sentences in the same discourse, we place a semi-colon between them; and in extreme cases, two sentences, each in every way grammatically complete, may be separated only by a comma. Thus the comma and semi-colon serve to show closeness of relationship as well as disconnection.

The conjunctions used to connect equals, which often appear in connecting two or more sentences to make a compound sentence, may have no punctuation mark before them, or a comma, or a semi-colon, or even a period, according to the closeness with which the sentences are associated in idea. These conjunctions are commonly *and, but,* and *or*, though some other conjunctions may be used in this way. *And* shows simple connection, the idea in the second sentence being simply added to the idea in the first. If the connection between the two sentences united by *and* is so close that we could hardly understand the first until we have comprehended the second, no comma should precede *and.* If one sentence is simply added to the other, each being tolerably complete in itself, a comma precedes *and.* This is the commonest usage. If we wish to show more disconnection than usual, we place a semi-colon before *and.* If *and* shows that the idea expressed in the sentence which follows it is an addition to all the ideas that go before, or to a general idea implied in several sentences, it must be preceded by a period, and of course be written with a capital letter.

But is disjunctive in its nature, and is used to indicate contrast. The separation between two sentences united by *but* is therefore normally greater than the separation indicated by *and*; and so *but* is usually preceded by a semi-colon. If we wish to indicate that the connection between the two sentences is a little closer than usual, we substitute a comma for the semi-colon; if the connection is very remote, or is with some idea expressed in several preceding sentences, *but* must begin with a capital letter and be preceded by a period.

Or follows the principles laid down for *and*.

7. The Dash and the Parenthesis

The dash indicates an abrupt change in the grammatical construction, or in the flow of the thought. When a wholly disconnected clause is thrown into a sentence it may be preceded and followed by a dash, or it may be enclosed within parentheses. Usually in place of a dash at each end we substitute the two parts of a parenthesis. The effect is the same.

The dash is often united with the comma. A comma and a dash are used in place of a colon in introducing a quotation in an easy and flowing manner, the colon being reserved for formal introductions. Formerly nearly all quotations were introduced by colons, but now the comma and dash are preferred in most cases.

Any abrupt change in the middle of a sentence is usually indicated by a comma and a dash.

Such phrases as "Dear sir" at the beginning of a letter may be followed either by a colon or by a comma and a dash. One method is as good as the other.

When a sentence is brought to an abrupt termination, being completely broken off, a dash of double length is used.

Examples: All this story was about____what do you think?

Well____don't know____that is____no, I cannot accept it.

"Gentlemen, I swear by all____" But the sentence was never finished.

The dash is also used in much the same way that the colon is, to indicate equality, especially in summarizing. Macaulay uses it in this way constantly.

Examples: Now, every man pursues his own happiness or interest—call it which you will.

They have already made the science of political economy—a science of vast importance to the welfare of the nations—an object of disgust.

For all possible checks may be classed under two heads,—want of will and want of power.

What Lord Bacon blames in the schoolmen is this,—that they reason syllogistically on words which had not been defined with precision.

A parenthetical clause within another of the same kind must be indicated by some other marks than those used to indicate the larger. We may alternate dashes and what are called marks of parenthesis, and in case of necessity we may use square brackets.

Brackets are regularly used to indicate words thrown into quotations by the writer who quotes. Sometimes these words are comments, sometimes words supplied to complete the meaning.

Example: Compare the following account of Lord Palmerston: "I have heard him [Lord Palmerston] say that he occasionally found that they [foreign ministers] had been deceived by the open manner in which he told them the truth."

When parenthetical words are not very different from

the text, dashes should be used; when the difference is greater, the round marks of parenthesis are to be employed; and brackets are to be used only when special occasion requires them.

8. Exclamation and Interrogation Points

Of course every direct question should be followed by a mark of interrogation, and every clear exclamation by an exclamation point.

Note that indirect questions are not followed by the interrogation point. *Example:* He asked me if I would go.

If interjections are used in connection with other words, the exclamation point should be placed only at the end of the whole exclamation. Each point denotes a separate exclamation. *Example:* Alas, I do not know where food is to be found!

Parts of sentences which lack either a subject or a predicate or both, if used at all, should be treated as exclamations and be followed by the exclamation point. *Example:* To think that I should do such a thing!

Whenever a direct question is raised, an interrogation point should indicate the fact. So sometimes we have an interrogation point enclosed in parenthesis, equivalent to an interrogative sentence, and after double dashes indicating that a sentence has come to an abrupt termination, the questioning intonation of the portion of the sentence given must be indicated by a question mark after the dash. The same rule applies to exclamations.

Example: "You were going to tell me____?" "Yes, I will tell you now."

9. The Hyphen

The hyphen is used at the end of a line when a word is broken off and a part of it is placed on the next line. Examples of this are common in every printed book. It is to be noted that the hyphen can never be placed at the beginning of the next line, as some uneducated people would place it. Moreover, a word can be broken only on a syllable, and the division of words into syllables as discussed under the head of "Word-Study" must be well understood if the hyphen is to be used correctly at the end of a line.

Hyphens are also used in compound words. When two words first unite they are commonly Joined by a hyphen. After a time the hyphen is omitted. Thus *police-man* once appeared in the dictionary with a hyphen, but it is never so written today. Usually it is necessary to refer to the dictionary to find out the proper way to write all compound words or words that may be compound. The black hyphen mark is used in the dictionary to indicate that the hyphen is always to be written, the light hyphen mark merely to divide the syllables.

Today, tomorrow, tonight, etc., are properly always written with the hyphen, though now-a-days many omit it.

When a noun is followed by a present participle, the whole forming a verbal noun, the noun and the participle are commonly united by a hyphen, as in the case of *story-writing, well-digging,* etc. An adjective preceding a verbal noun (present participle), or indeed any noun, should never be united to that noun by a hyphen.

When one noun preceded by an adjective is used as a sort of compound adjective, the two words (noun and adjective) are united by the hyphen. *For example: common sense* used as a noun and adjective should never be united in any way, either by a hyphen or by being written as one word. But *common-sense reasoning* is phrase in which the noun sense united with its adjective becomes itself an adjective. In the case of *short story writing*, our principles would require a hyphen between *story* and *writing* and also between *short* and *story*. But this would make a combination too long to be elegant, and so the hyphen should properly be omitted in both cases.

When one noun is used as a sort of adjective before another noun, a hyphen is used if the combination is close, but if it is not close no hyphen is used. We write *apple-tree*, but *stone fence*. The latest usage is against the hyphen in such cases.

10. Other Marks

Every exact quotation should be enclosed within quotation marks. A quotation within a quotation is enclosed within single marks, and a quotation within that by double marks again.

Example: "Said he, 'Can you tell me what "Cut it out" means?'

Slang words or phrases for which the writer does not care to take personal responsibility may be included within quotation marks, as "Cut it out" in the preceding example.

An apostrophe is not only used as the sign of the possessive case of nouns, but also to indicate any omission of letters in a word, as in the abbreviations "I'll" for "I will," "ne'er" for "never," etc.

When a few words are left out of a quotation, the

places where the omissions are made are filled with two or three periods, or with stars. These signs are most commonly required in making long quotations which must be condensed.

Reference to notes is usually indicated by a star. When there are several notes on the same page, the star is used for the first note, the single dagger usually for the second, the double dagger for the third, and after that two stars, the sign for the paragraph, or other signs may be used as taste dictates. When the notes exceed three it is usually better to employ small superior figures.

In writing, the sign of the paragraph may be prefixed to the first word of a sentence which the writer wishes especially to indicate as the beginning of a new paragraph. This sign is common when indentation has been forgotten or over-looked, or is not sufficiently clear.

The use of special signs will be found fully explained at the back of Webster's dictionary.

Conclusion

For the student who wishes to gain skill in punctuation, it is believed that the brief statement of principles and examples here given will be of more value than a fuller treatment of the subject. The chief thing is that the student should form the habit of observing the punctuation in his reading of modern standard literature. It is only in this way that the instinct can be trained, and instinct alone will usually suffice for the multifarious cases which must constantly arise in actual practice.

As an exercise, examine the selections from standard authors contained in this work, trying to decide in your own mind just why each punctuation mark was used. A faithful study of this kind, continued through fifty or a hundred pages, a page or two at a time, cannot but prove more instructive than any amount of study of rules. After such a study, a test of ability may be made by copying such passages, omitting all punctuation marks, capital letters, etc., and when the marks have been forgotten, writing out the passage with all the marks included. This may then be compared with the original, and useful lessons will be learned. When the latter of these exercises can be executed quite without error, there is excellent evidence that the art of punctuation has been mastered. Masters of literature selected for such practice should be very modern, since usage in punctuation has changed somewhat in a hundred and even in forty or fifty years.* But except for this variation, any alteration in punctuation indicates an alteration in meaning, just as much as any alteration in words. There are not two ways to punctuate the same passage and still convey exactly the same meaning.

* Commas were used much more freely fifty years ago than they are today, and so were capitals.